head hooligan

...SHE IS YOU

LYNETTE HEYWOOD

Fisher King Publishing

HEAD HOOLIGAN... SHE IS YOU

Published by
Fisher King Publishing
www.fisherkingpublishing.co.uk

To My Head Hooligan

Her inner voice, the restless rogue who clatters around her brain
An overthinker whose dreams outran the quiet life,
whose peace feels far from plain

At midnights edge, when stars start to lose their glow
The Head Hooligan unchains her jangling mind

A dance of doubt, reels of yes and no
and of should haves that she's left behind
Or might have been's that are hard to find

She'll toss beneath her sheets in tangled thought
Where every whisper's loud, each question tall
From moments, she remembers, but forgot to let go.

Yet here's the truth she's come to see at last
This Head Hooligan is her, her shadow and her space

The voice that pulls her back to look at the past
but also dares her to be wild and always lights her face

So now she holds her chaos like a friend
a dance with fear with dreams she'd never planned

No longer just a nuisance she'd upend
But one she loves and strives to understand

The Head Hooligan won't hush, she just won't let her be
But they're one heart, two halves, a fierce duet

And in this sleepless breathless reverie,
she found herself imperfect and unset

Thank you, for she is me.

Contents

Introduction

I would like to welcome you and show my appreciation that you have picked up my book; thank you.

This book is for all you overthinkers, who can't sleep because of the thoughts going round in your head but also…

To the gorgeous girl who, like most of us, has struggled at some points of her life yet has had to battle on regardless. To the lovely lady who has spent sleepless nights worrying herself sick, overthinking thoughts that she feels she can't control. This book is for the wonderful woman who feels exhausted daily, yet because 'exhaustion' isn't in the calendar, but a period is, as is getting the kids to school or that full day of hard graft with the dread of the misogynistic boss who insults her constantly throughout the day, on she plods.

I wrote it for the beautifully matured, confused girl, (yeah *girl*, because she is always there within you) who has already had enough hot sweats to last her a lifetime and can't understand why her belly all of a sudden looks like the four pound of tripe she used to buy her grandad from the butchers. Of course, that's not the case, ladies, your belly is beautiful whatever it looks like, you just have to believe it.

It's for you, the woman who knows that the struggle is real enough but often told to 'Get on with it' or 'You've got this' and whose response wants to be 'I don't want this!' The insecure ladies, who feel like they never properly fit in. Those who view social media and compare it to their own lives. And the other women who stand at the school gate, wondering how all the other mums are so confident.

What do you all have in common? You do your best every day to paint on a smile and as act normal as you can in public.

How *do* you do it? How do you get through your day at times and how *do* you manage that beautiful smile with only your eyes telling the truth? If people stopped and took time maybe they'd see the truth in your eyes, but in all honesty, so many of us feel like this, so caught up in our own lives, that we don't actually notice what other people's eyes are saying to us.

It's so goddamn hard at times.

It's also for you beautiful mums who feel like you've had enough, but with treacle on your feet you get up – often with one breast hanging out and sick in your hair – and feed your baby. Doing this whilst so bogged down in the relationship with the childlike father who just won't commit to this new role. I *know* that most dads are amazing (mine was), but I hear enough tales that would make your eyes water from our girls who end up going it alone. If you have a new baby and feel like the father isn't committing, you aren't alone. As if the sleepless nights are not enough, as your hormones are raging, plus any trauma you've been through delivering this bundle of joy, it's certainly not helpful if you have got some arsehole telling you, 'You're a shit mum' or to 'Get a grip as loads of women have babies!' Maybe you're feeling almost an element of regret, fuelled with pain and PPD (postpartum depression) to boot.

There are so many scenarios I could go through where the woman is always left 'dealing' with the shit or left traumatised through trusting someone they shouldn't. So many occasions where she could have given up, gone to bed and hidden from the world.

I could write three or four books if I jotted them all down. But I know the anxiety and pain these scenarios can cause and, because you are a woman, and you *have* to get on with it, because of the demands placed on us, we can't hide away from the world, so you end up juggling it all, *but* even Superwoman can't live on that energy, something has to give.

My book is for all of you, but the lady who I resonate with the most (albeit I could fit into all the above scenarios) is the one that overthinks, panics, has anxious thoughts and feelings, starts to act differently, doesn't sleep, and is absolutely exhausted living this circular habit of negativity that she can't seem to break free from. Not forgetting the woman who is working ridiculous hours and doesn't have any respect from her boss but feels trapped in her job…

Anyway, this book is not a one-size-fits-all, there are too many variations of us. It's for every woman out there, who may feel overwhelmed with life or who is wanting to make a change. I've written this for others who may lie awake at night with thoughts like little hooligans swirling through their minds, causing chaos and not giving them any rest – you're not alone, I have a Head Hooligan too (I'll introduce you to her later, you might actually like her and could grow to like yours too. Honestly!)

I have often thought, 'Bollocks, I can't take anymore' as I have tried to justify it all by stating, 'Life only throws at you that, what you can handle!' Well, there comes a point when we don't want to handle it anymore, thanks. And for those who are told that 'it'll make you stronger!' I can honestly say, the Hulk looks like a weakling compared to me! So, we don't need any more tips on how to be strong, thank you very much!

You've probably picked up this book because, like me, you're wanting to be a better *you*.

You want to be rid of the horrendous feelings of

anxiety, which can cause you physical pain. You'd love to put a stop to that constant negative chatter in your head. You want to stop pleasing people, because in doing this you resent others and yourself for being so goddamn accommodating and you want to clear your life of toxic people (easier said than done, hey?), or you want to learn how to deal with them and their drama that's so easy to become embroiled in.

You're here with me and if you read on, you will see I can help you find ways to make even the smallest of changes that will enable *you* to start making the difference which *will* help you feel better.

I am a qualified life coach and have counselling qualifications. I also have a qualification in PTSD (Post Traumatic Stress Disorder). I'm not a doctor or a psychiatrist. I'm more self-taught on how our minds create our own story and nightmares, and I'm experienced in having internal meltdowns, smiling whilst nodding my head to please every *fucker* that comes my way (*sorry for the language*) and then kicking myself afterwards for not being honest, and instead nodding away.

With experiences like this I hope I can show you that you're not alone and it *is* possible to overcome the most challenging of times.

My people-pleasing has caused me no end of distress

in the past. I never actually *wanted* to please *everyone*, sometimes I wanted to tell everybody to get lost, but I couldn't. It's almost like it's my makeup, it's me, but because I'm aware now of where it comes from and that I do it for acceptance, through fear of being rejected, it makes it easier for me to deal with. I still nod more than I'd like to, though, but saying 'no' isn't as tough anymore.

Confession – you're not going to finish the last page in this book and be like, 'Oh it's gone, I no longer have a Head Hooligan, she's gone away!' But this book will help you realise that you're not alone and that actually you can start to feel a bit better about who you are and why. There is a way to stop negative thoughts by helping your Head Hooligan to become positive, you can actually learn to like her!

Although, I will say this – to realise it you have to *hear* it. When you *hear* it, you have to *feel* it. And once you've *felt* it… you will *hear* me.

You have to realise too, that you do have a problem and that it's *not* the people around you, nor is it the big bad world, as difficult as it all is right now… it is you.

I know, it's not nice to be told that **you** are the problem, but it's empowering. Once you know the problem sits within you, it gives you the ability to change it, to tackle the problem, to find solutions and become happier. Honestly!

Also, because even though we think we can, we actually can't concentrate on two things at once so we should stop trying to do so. I can see so many of you now, trying it out in your head, but try as you might it's not possible. OK, OK, so you can rub your head and pat your belly, or whichever way round it goes, but you put two of your favourite songs on at the same time and try to listen to them... you will not be able to listen to them both. My point is, if you concentrate on reading and do nothing else – forget those pots piling up in the sink and get that TV off so there is no noisy background – it will give your mind a break. It will help.

It will, if nothing else, distract you from your own Head Hooligan who makes the inner noise that plagues your beautiful mind. It will give you a bit of 'me time', something we all deserve massively. It also might help you to cope a bit better and become more aware of yourself, which would be amazing.

I've written this book because I care, I genuinely care. If I could take the pain away for every suffering woman, then I honestly would. If I could stop all the negative overthinking that we do, I would. If I could make you realise that you're wasting so much of your beautiful time overthinking, then my purpose here on Earth is done. So, please, if you take one tiny thing from this then it'll be worth every hour, I've spent typing it.

Back to me. I am an author of three published drama books (writing is my therapy) and the world's biggest overthinker – I have a resident Head Hooligan. My Head Hooligan has shared my head from the moment I could talk but has become prominent over the last ten years or so. At times taking over and making such a racket there I've felt compelled to go inside and physically drag her out. I am *or was* a habitual, addicted, overthinker. *Every* day I have to work hard to get my thoughts to a stable realistic place in order for me to succeed in my life. Don't worry, having a Head Hooligan doesn't mean I have psychosis, she's purely my inner monologue, but she gets bloody carried away with obsessive, negative, over-thinking thoughts.

I know there are thousands of women out there who also have a Head Hooligan, or if you don't have one yet, there is a chance you could do in the future. I thought if I introduced you to mine it could help you in calming yours, because I totally understand what you're going through. And hopefully, like me, you'll come to a point where the thoughts in your head are mostly positive.

I've read a thousand self-help books, some of spiritual meaning, others on psychology. I did a course in PTSD. It has been a great help in understanding what is going on in my own head as well as in the minds of others. All of these gave me the same message, but each time I was looking for that immediate fix – I expected with each book to finish it and feel totally free.

I was missing the message.

There was a time in my life when I became totally desperate, desperate for my Head Hooligan to go away and desperate for me to understand why I plagued myself like this.

I was constantly playing past events in my head and wondering if I should have done 'this' or I shouldn't have done 'that'. Even happy events that I should have been excited about, my Head Hooligan would be there sucking every bit of excitement out of me and replacing it with angst. Future events would leave me catastrophising about the day ahead. Me and my Head Hooligan were the best *team*, by this I mean the best team in making my thoughts so much bigger than they actually were. I would take them to bed with me, I'd toss and turn in a hot sweat, actually arguing with her all the time, sometimes becoming so angry with her that I could have literally punched myself in the head.

If I did eventually drift off, my Head Hooligan would come with me, and I would have terrible nightmares. My sleep was becoming disrupted and there was no break from it. Sleep is supposed to be soothing, but there were times when my dreams were that bad, I was aware even in sleep that my anxiety was still with me. It was circular because the next day I would feel beyond knackered and start my day a shaky mess and magnifying even more my anxiety.

Maybe you don't relate to this, and you think totally differently. That's OK. You can still learn and grow from what I have to share with you. Maybe in reading this you'll realise more about yourself or someone you know. It could give you an insight into why your mother behaved a certain way or why a friend is needing your support. Of course, not everyone has this inner dialogue – there is evidence that some people think in colours and shapes and not words and don't have an internal voice, and some people with anxiety fall asleep straight away, but reading about those of us who do experience these things, can help give you an insight into what it is like.

It's taken a lot of reading and working through my courses to get to a better me. I have taken one main thing, one main lesson out of it all. A lesson which has made me start to turn it around. I admit, I have not yet done a full 360, but *awareness is the key for the treasure that is actually buried in your own head*. There are lots of other lessons, of course, but this for me did it, even though I had read about it a thousand times, I had to hear it and I had to feel it.

I had to be aware.

'*If you change the way you look at things, the things you look at change.*' A quote by one of my favourite self-help authors, Dr Wayne Dyer. This man, in my darkest hours, was my light. I became obsessed with his books. I would find the internal space (so difficult amongst my own internal non-stop chatter) to slow down, listen and take them in. It's difficult to concentrate when you're feeling anxious, but I found that a good source for this is audiobooks. I am a reader who has always loved to have a book in my hands, the *smell* of the cover, the f*eel* of the pages. An audiobook was a new way of helping the *words* sink in and every spare minute I had, I would pop my Air Pods in and listen away.

In parallel, I was doing my course on PTSD, and I could hear Wayne's words and quotes and thought, 'My god he's right!' My course spoke about therapies such as CBT (Cognitive Behaviour Therapy). CBT is a good tool to use to help you deal with overwhelming problems in a more positive way by breaking them down into smaller parts and looking at those smaller parts differently. '*If you change the way you look at things, the things you look at change.*'

It's the same with another of my favourite self-help speakers/authors, Louise Hay, who has a very spiritual approach to her messages. I would find her positive affirmations on YouTube and play them in the background as I was getting ready for the hard slog that is work. In all honesty, I used to have a much better day for doing so.

It is said that positive affirmations fire up your neural pathways and make changes to the areas of the brain that make you happy and positive.

This wonderful lady has helped so many people or, correction (as she wouldn't be happy with that statement), she has guided people to help themselves. Reading her book, *You Can Heal Your Life* was another turning point for me getting on the right path.

I now have a lovely, happy life and want for nothing. This certainly doesn't mean that I live in a palace and have a big pot of endless money. I still have to work; I have bills like the rest of you. But my changes in life have been more about my attitude towards it and realising that as long as I'm safe and well, can breathe every day, have my gorgeous family around me, what more *could* I want?

I worry less now about things I can't control. That bit *has* turned around nearly a full 360 because, believe me, life as I know it now hasn't always been like this. And by turning my Head Hooligan into my Head Buddy, I have created a whole new meaning for myself. There are still days she attacks me, but I know how to manage it all a lot better. Always remember that worries only exist if you let them.

I've been in debt, constantly borrowing money from anyone who would lend it to me. I've dealt with bailiffs and other debt collectors. I'd refuse to pay any bills or would pay a bit off at a time and would stress myself out so much when they just kept mounting up. I lived on the edge by getting paid for working bloody hard, blowing my money and then borrowing for the rest of the month.

Until one day, I realised that it was *me* and *my* relationship with money that brought on the debt and *not* the world around me. I've always earnt good money, I just never knew that I had a massive fear of it and never thought I had enough no matter what my bank account looked like. I now have savings and an excellent credit score for the first time ever.

Just by changing my attitude.

The running of my homes had always been a disaster. I was never able to keep them nice. I would leave décor in a state for years and then, of course, I had no money. So, I always blamed the state of my house on a lack of money. Like my mind, my house was always in a state of chaos, that in itself was stressful for me and my children. When I learnt that it was *me*, I looked at my previous homes and was almost pissed off and angry that I'd done that, that I'd never taken any pride in my homes and just seen them as a burden. I now have a lovely home, in a wonderful area, and I've not missed a monthly payment for years.

I was addicted to food and was overweight thus making me unhealthy and unhappy, and again I later realised that *fear* was leading me. I was turning to food to help me mask the real problems. I thought about food all the time, and when I wasn't thinking about it, I was eating it. She had a lot to answer for as she sat in my head grinning, calling me a fat bastard. I'd almost eat to spite my Head Hooligan. You can just see her, can't you, sitting there demure, nibbling on bloody lettuce?

I never dealt with what was happening in my life; I'd just have a big fat chippy with five slices of bread instead. It made my self-loathing worse as I got bigger. It was a form of self-harm. I would eat, not even enjoying the food because I knew that I was going to hate myself once I felt stuffed and unable to move. I now don't even think about it anymore, I very rarely diet, and my weight is stable.

Almost every relationship I had was unhealthy, I seemed to attract the same 'something' in men. I would be the ultimate pleaser, the fixer and the doer. So, I was constantly used or felt used. I always ended up with

Mr Needy but subconsciously thinking it was great for validation because they thought I was amazing. So, I'd go for someone with issues, or someone I thought I could fix, but ultimately it always wore thin with me in the end as I was left feeling exasperated, unloved and desperately searching for more and more validation as I failed to fix *them*.

Then I hit the lowest of the low and, through my own self-loathing, allowed *someone* in who did me so much damage that I am still recovering.

That was the catalyst for my Head Hooligan's malfunction.

I've got it right now and met my equal who gives me as much as I give him, who does as much (if not more) than I do, who wants to grow with me as we encourage each other in every step the other one is taking. My fear of rejection in relationships is still there, don't get me wrong, but I'm aware – totally and utterly aware. As we book our third holiday this year, I am so grateful because there really was a time, not so long ago, when I'd be liking other people's holiday pics on Facebook, thinking to myself and believing that holidays for me were a thing of the past.

I have changed the way I look at things and my life is… incredibly different.

I still and always will have bad days and bad nights,

but I deal with them all so differently now and my attacks don't last for long. I no longer berate my Head Hooligan or beat myself up for when she becomes a Head Hooligan. I have learnt how to tame her, by making her my Head Buddy. Why *should* your own thoughts be so cruel to you? They should be kind like a Buddy. But we have to know how to do it.

When she's your Head Buddy, life becomes so much easier.

I don't dread things such as future events anymore, well not like I used to, because now I don't think about the trigger, I breathe easily through all that is approaching, and you can too.

In this book I'll share my story, but I don't want any sympathy because I am not a victim. I'm far from it. I just want you to hear my journey, yours will be different. Your journey may not be as dramatic or monumental and that's OK. You don't have to have gone through debt problems, self-harm or catastrophic relationships to feel trauma and to be struggling with Head Hooligans. Or you *could* have had catastrophic events happen to you, you might be dealing with terrible loss, or dealing with realising your childhood wasn't what it seemed. Whatever your story is, never play your overthinking down. I know how debilitating it can be, no matter what it looks like for you on the outside.

I'll share how I changed my thoughts and how I learnt to look at things differently. I'll share some tools that have helped me massively.

I'll go through the main areas that lead to the way you're feeling and how the negative thoughts you're having create pain and anxiety, and how pain and anxiety cause you to overthink and catastrophise.

Hopefully you'll relate because I know that life isn't easy – especially when you're an overthinking woman. What I'm hoping to do is help you turn your negative thoughts into nice ones, so that if you do have a busy brain that struggles to shut down, together we will make sure we turn your Head Hooligan into your Head Buddy, it's such better company to have around.

"I'm not sure which is worse:
intense feeling, or the absence of it."

Margaret Attwood

Chapter One - Her Overthinking

Overthinking is when we engage in negative thought processes; for which there seems no end. The thoughts are almost on a continuous loop that go round and round in your head. This can be such a distressing experience for the lady trying to deal with everything else in conjunction.

Rumination is the term used by psychologists and is when we replay the same thoughts over and over in our heads. We usually ruminate about the past. There was once a need for this when you were cave woman, because you would have had to be alert at all times. If you had just escaped a sabre tooth tiger, your mind would have gone into *life and death* mode, and you would have replayed the scenario in your head over and over to prevent the scenario happening again or at least plan how to escape the sabre tooth tiger again.

Nowadays we don't need it as much, but the brain still sometimes thinks that first meeting you had with 'his' friends that you 'messed up' is still a life-or-death scenario, so it plays it over and over trying to get it right for you, but we don't need it anymore so it's unhelpful and damaging to constantly replay your past. Even though we *don't* need it anymore there is no bloody switch to switch it off, or no label saying 'no longer in use' to stick over it.

We *do* need thought though; we need thought to help us make decisions, we need thought to get us through our lives. It's overthinking thoughts that take over and don't tell the truth, which we don't need. Sometimes you're not just playing them over and over again and ruminating, you also start to add in your own dramatic scenes. And, unless there are any Sofia Coppolas amongst us, our own scenes are shite, scary, unhelpful and can leave us reeling. They're also a waste of time and unconstructive.

For example, I used to regularly travel to London for work (I still do but not as often). I was there a few days before the bombing that struck the transport network in July 2005.

Years later if I had to travel, I'd overthink it so much in the days leading up to it, I'd not be able to sleep. Instead, I would be overthinking all the disasters that had happened to people in London, or anywhere, by being in the wrong place at the wrong time.

I'd catastrophise my whole journey – from getting on a train that derailed after a knifeman ran rampage up and down the carriages, to being stuck on a tube because a bomb had gone off.

I would ruminate about scenarios that included me actually being there on that dreadful day in 2005 and what would have happened if I'd have stayed on in London for a few days extra. My Head Hooligan would thrive on my tossing and turning by telling me that next time I had to go to London I was going and not coming back.

The whole process would leave me standing on the platform waiting for the 6am to Euston shaking, a mushy head and feeling that knackered that I literally didn't care about the day ahead. I'd be worn out.

You can see from that example how I overthought, catastrophised and ruminated myself into exhaustion, leaving myself in a state of dread. Even if I wasn't due in London for another week it would take over the entire week and I wouldn't be properly living or present.

I know my own overthinking has left me short of wanting the world to stop so I can get off at times. I can't stop the world, though. I have to carry on. I'm a mum. I have a job and a partner so it's impossible to even contemplate giving up. I've had dreams of living off-grid, so I can't be affected by today's world and the people in it that constantly cause me aggro in my head. I've since learnt that it's actually *me* that causes the aggro in my head.

Why? Because I continued to house my own little Head Hooligan.

I know that, like me, most women will wear a mask, Cat Woman has nothing on us!

I have worn my mask better than anyone; from the

outside I look like I've never had to deal with anything out of the ordinary, I'm confident and I'm on it, and I've never had to drag my belly off the floor as it bolts internally with nerves.

Ladies, how often do you want to take that mask off and just be you for a while? But instead, you keep your mask on. You hide all the overthinking you're doing.

I don't believe that overthinking is recognised as a mental health condition, but it can be a symptom of depression, anxiety and OCD (Obsessive Compulsive Disorder).

Recent studies have shown that overthinking comes from trauma. This could be trauma experienced as a child or even something perceived to be a trauma later on in life.

We'll cover trauma later; you'll be surprised at what can be classed as such. There are some little things which can happen in life which you may never have even realised causes trauma. I know that's where my overthinking certainly came from, and it does make sense now I understand it a bit more.

Overthinking is a destroyer; it will destroy everything in its path, including you. It's like you're constantly waiting for something that never happens. Your critical thoughts (your Head Hooligan) cling on to any mistakes you've made and force you to berate yourself by replaying them. Overthinking can become physical at times too; your belly can feel in knots, and you can taste bile. It can cause other physical symptoms such as gut problems, ulcers, jaw ache and chest pains.

It's circular because overthinking causes us pain and the pain subsequently causes us to overthink.

I want to write a couple of examples of me and how I overthink; instead, I'm sitting here trying to think of an example of me overthinking and I have procrastinated and can't think of a single example now. What if you ladies think that I am making all this up just to write a book?! So, what's the point? What if my thoughts on paper look really trivial?

Back on track we go!

My first example: At work.

I once had to send an email at work. It was a response to one that had been sent to me and I was feeling anxious.

I'd not been in my job for long so was ultra-sensitive about everything I did. I wanted to make a good impression, and, because of past trauma, I was craving acceptance – my fear of rejection could send me spiralling. The dose of imposter syndrome wasn't helping either. *What am I doing here? Am I a fraud? I can't do this!*

Early on in my new job, every night I'd get into bed and replay my day, creating terrible scenes – usually about how my colleagues were perceiving me in my new role.

Anyway, after I had all the relevant information of the required email typed out, I read it and read it and read it. Honestly the screen became blurry as I'd spent so long looking over this one email, so anxious to get it 'right'.

Then, I got one of the guys to check it for me, just to make sure I had all the correct information. I even went to another one of the guys and triple checked with them that I had my information right. You may think this was a very important email, but it was only a very simple one requiring a short response.

My fear of rejection was going round and round my head. *If I get something wrong, I will be exposed to the whole business in a bad light. They will know I'm that little girl from that huge council estate who wore odd socks to school. They won't think I can do this job. Colleagues will then KNOW that I shouldn't be working at this level, because they KNOW I am thick really and I have no education to back me up!*

My Head Hooligan didn't help in convincing me otherwise. *'They will wonder how you got to where you are today!'*

I began overthinking even more. *Why am I in this job?*

Maybe it's my personality and people like me… or maybe they feel sorry for me!

'No, they know you're fake!' Head Hooligan continued.

Then all I could think about was what would happen if I *did* make a mistake on this email. I couldn't see any logic; that sometimes we all make mistakes. All I could then do was think about mistakes I'd made in the past.

I once sent a response in the wrong Team's Chat, so the incorrect group of people received a message that made no sense to them whatsoever. Their responses were coming through thick and fast, and my anxiety was kicking in; but I cleared it up and it was over in seconds.

However, as I sat waiting to send this email, I kept replaying that incident with the Team's Chat and imagining all that could have happened if the message I'd sent had contained other information – personal details or confidential information. I felt hot sweats beginning.

My Head Hooligan, sitting demurely, enjoying me panicking, reminded me that I could always ask my old boss for my old job back.

I felt even more panicky. *Maybe I should start trawling through job sites looking for a lower paid role that I'd be good at…*

Eventually I sent the email, after an entire day worrying, overthinking and ruminating over it. The email was all fine, it got the response that was needed, and nobody questioned the content. I'd spent a whole day on that email, listening to my Head Hooligan.

Now, when something like that happens, I allow my Head Hooligan to speak, but I ask her to be kind to me. I let her be kind to me as she points out that she helps me rewire my brain.

'You are good at what you do.

You're an author, for God's sake, you can *write.*

You don't need validation from others.

You're dead clever.'

AND YES, YES, I'M AN AUTHOR, of course I can write an email. I now hear her positives.

Now she gives me the confidence to fire off emails all day, but if I do need help, I know it's OK to ask.

I am where I am because I've worked hard. I lead from within and holistically. The guys know that we're one team. They have confidence in me that I'd never let them do anything that I wouldn't do. Encouraging them and empowering them all the time, we work hard, and we play hard.

But to realise this, I have to almost have myself in an 'emotional headlock', trying to get my subconscious to record that *I am good enough,* by constantly telling myself that I am.

Another example: A personal one.

My partner, who I love dearly, supports me daily but only sees the tip of my iceberg at times. Before I accepted me for being me, I'd hardly share any of my thoughts and keep them between me and my Head Hooligan, in case he left me or had me sectioned. He didn't and wouldn't, of course, but there I go again.

We've not shared a bad word between each other yet, and we're seven years in. His actions are beyond any words that can say how much he loves me. He shows me constantly.

Yet, when we first moved in together, he would come home from work on occasions in a serious mood. I say serious because I'm yet to see him in a bad mood. He would clearly have been tired from doing his 12-hour shift, as none of us are getting any younger and he's allowed to be in any bloody mood he wants. Because I'd not seen this mood when we were dating, my Head Hooligan, determined to make me believe I was unlovable, would chant my bloody narrative.

He'd be five minutes through the door; and I'd feel it and that's it, I'd be on it.

'It's you. He never used to be like this, he's changed

his mind – he doesn't want to live with you.'

So, after the initial hot sweat and belly ache had attacked me, her chants would make the hot sweats and belly ache worse, until I literally would need to go to the toilet.

Head Hooligan would turn to rumination (she's bloody clever, you know).

'Well how was he when he called you this morning? You probably were off with him. Did you offend him?'

She'd have me going over the phone conversation trying to remember every word, replaying it in my mind, changing it each time to try and find some bad words between us and second-guess me offending him.

After I had kicked myself to death with that one, I would start to look for another reason that he was in this mood rather than him doing cartwheels and licking my bloody face.

'It's because he's just been in the bathroom and your pyjamas are still on the floor from last night. You are so untidy; he will be thinking what a dirty cow you are!'

I'd bloody run upstairs and start cleaning the bastard bathroom, berating myself for being so untidy (forgetting that I'd worked all day and that actually he didn't give a shit what was on the bathroom floor, because if he did... he'd pick it up).

Bathroom spotless and the phone call out of my head, I was just about to breathe when he would close the kitchen door a big harder than normal. And then I'd be sure I could hear Head Hooligan jumping up and down with glee in my head.

'That's it, he's simply had enough of you, he knows you're off your head and he wants better, he wants more fun, he wants a sexy young girl, you're premenopausal! HE'S HAVING AN AFFAIR. You need to give him more attention. And don't do that high-pitched voice because you know you've already asked him six times how his day was.'

I'd allowed my Head Hooligan to get me so worked up that she'd actually convinced me (albeit for a minute) that I needed to start looking for somewhere else to live. After I'd berated my whole appearance.

Jeez, am I wearing you out? Because I'm sitting here shaking my head as I read back, but I know that loads of other women will think like this too.

The poor man had not uttered a derogatory word. He just didn't come in from work doing cartwheels or licking my ear, but he'd cooked dinner as he does every night.

There was no problem, other than *me.*

Of course, there will be times that a woman is worried about her man and that maybe he is cheating and it's important not to dismiss it, but that will come with way more signs than just a slight frown as he walks through the door. I'm not dismissing that sometimes there *are* problems. I'm merely pointing out that for the overthinker, something as simple as a frown can give your Head Hooligan a green light to start her merry dance.

I'm thankful that I reacted inwardly and not outwardly at times, as I know how mad I would sound if I had spoken what I was thinking.

Now, when my Head Hooligan arrives and says, 'He's frowning, he doesn't like you!' I say, 'Right, lady, you're my Head Buddy now, remember to be kind.' I hear her little cough of recognition, her tone changes as she reminds me:

'He frowns sometimes, and he looks sexy.

You have a beautiful relationship, built on friendship, you talk about everything, laugh over anything and are the best team.'

It's almost like I've rewired my brain, because when I look back at those days, I know now it was the PTSD taking over. I no longer worry, instead I ask a caring, supportive question about his day and leave the pyjamas where they belong… on the bathroom floor! As a result, I'm much calmer now and in control.

My third and final example – the worries of being a mother, but of course my Head Hooligan takes it to the extreme…

My youngest son found gathering with friends was more fun than sitting at home – a natural progression in life.

But, my God, when he went to his first festival…

I was anxious anyway because he's my youngest and he wasn't as forthcoming with communicating as the others (although recently he's become great at phoning Mum).

Before I got in bed, I made a decision that I wouldn't text him or bother him as he would be having fun. I was determined to sleep for a couple of hours, planning to wake up when he was due in. Then I could worry if I needed to.

Anyway, I went to bed, trying to forget about him.

In total retaliation with myself I sent him a text as I knew the final acts of the night would be nearly finishing. I checked my phone over 100 times and there was no response to my text. Then when I looked closer, I saw that it hadn't been delivered.

I was hot and sweaty with fear. I was now staring at the phone, checking for the 'delivered' notification and it wasn't coming.

By midnight, I was literally going to throw up because old Winnie the Witch, aka my Head Hooligan, was head-to-head with me, or so it felt.

'You know he's been attacked, and his phone has been stolen.'

Unfortunately, I went through the scenario with her egging me on. Step by step I went through every mother's nightmare. The visions in my head were becoming unbearable as I imagined him getting attacked. I was creating my own nightmare. The internal turmoil was rife. I'd try to stop the thoughts, but I was too deep within them, and I couldn't.

My Head Hooligan was having a field day.

'Even if he hasn't been attacked, if he's lost his phone he could be stuck.

How will he get home?

He will walk all the way from Warrington, you know what will happen then?

He'll be drunk and he will lie in a bush and sleep, and…'

I got up and went downstairs. I began pacing up and down the living room, checking that bastard phone constantly, dripping in sweat.

When I got to his funeral in my head and the tears were rolling down my face, I berated myself. *You're an absolute idiot! You're going to manifest it; this will happen if you keep thinking like this.*

I was totally and utterly mentally exhausted at this point.

Then of course, as I'm sitting sobbing in the living room, he came in. He'd lost his phone and was devastated. But I was just so relieved to see him, I didn't care that he had lost his phone, it wasn't important as long as he was safe.

And the day after? I was a walking zombie. My Cat Woman mask was on my arse and not my face. And my son blissfully slept off his first festival.

Now, when I start to worry, I say to my Head Hooligan, "Please, please be kind tonight as he's going out again.'

She is kind and states:

'He's such a sensible kid.

He always gets home in one piece.

It must be easier now you're a bit more used to it.

He's just having a good time. If anything did happen, you would be contacted by one of his friends.'

The more I tell her to be kind, the more I am rewiring my brain to think more positively, which takes away my fears and makes me feel so much better.

Are you still with me? Can you relate this?

Can you see the common theme amongst my three

examples?

Nothing bad happened, the only thing that happened each and every time was that I let my Head Hooligan take over and she had a ball, causing nothing but unnecessary pain, sickness and exhaustion in all three scenarios.

In my examples I was actually **catastrophising;** it's another symptom of anxiety and depression possibly caused again through trauma. When we catastrophise our thinking becomes distorted, and we see an unfavourable outcome to an event and jump to the worst possible conclusion without any evidence. Even a situation that is naturally worrying (like your son being at a festival) will always end in disaster for the catastrophiser, i.e., your partner leaving you, losing your job, or your kid dying every time he/she leaves their bedroom.

The important detail in all three scenarios is: *nothing bad happened,* the bad thoughts didn't come into fruition, and they never have. Although bad things *do* happen, they're not usually the ones you've catastrophised about and it certainly doesn't help by overthinking about them either.

So that's me and my Head Hooligan in a snapshot. The examples I've given are the milder ones, she really can take it to the extreme. It may seem trivial to some of you, you may even think, 'Wow, just get on with it and *stop* thinking like that!' There will be others who may think, 'Bloody hell, her Head Hooligan and mine are best mates!'

All of these scenarios robbed me of my time and happiness and just *being*. I've wasted so much time thinking of negatives that I even went through a kind of grief imagining my son dead. Why would I put myself through *grief* like that?

After I had been diagnosed with PTSD and was embarking on a journey of trying to make friends with my Head Hooligan, the amount of time I was wasting hit me when I went to a beautiful lady's funeral. Her eulogy was amazing, her daughters stood up and told the story of her life. I actually felt jealous of the life that she had and how wonderful and bloody loved she was.

I got home that evening and thought about my own eulogy and what it would be like (of course I did, it's in the overthinking manual, my bloody Head Hooligan was sitting there, pen poised), in fact I've probably written my own eulogy in my head more times than a Eulogist.

I realised that if it were my funeral, the church *would* be full of love and that my eulogy *would* be amazing too. So, I started to add more gratitude into my life.

As a little girl I always dreamed of having a stage which I could do whatever I wanted on. I would dance and sing or read for my pretend audience; they adored me. It always made me feel amazing because I'd imagine that everyone would think I was beautiful and so, so clever.

It hit me hard; my funeral would be the only day that I would be centre of that stage and that was the only time I would know that people loved me and thought I was beautiful and... actually, I wouldn't know because I'd be fricking dead.

I needed to wake up to what was around me, that people do love me (of course some probably hate me too) and some people do think I'm amazing. I'm already on that stage... the stage of life. I didn't need to wait for my funeral to prove it.

I couldn't change it right away. But I could try. First of all, I needed to work even harder and quit my addiction to overthinking and stop the thoughts, because in having them I realised that I was missing something crucial; I was missing my journey, and I was missing what was really going on in my life. I had to stop my Head Hooligan running my life and my thoughts. This was my life, and I could run it myself! Easy-peasy right!?

Now that I knew I wanted to start living my life and taking it for what it was, it was time to find out where it all came from and why I was in this state of such a negative flow. Surely that would help with proper healing.

How many times have you asked for this?

*"Peace of mind for five minutes,
that's what I crave."*

Alanis Morissette

Chapter Two - Why She Lives in Fear

It is thought that overthinking and catastrophising have been linked with trauma, or PTSD. When a world of fear is born, the result is that past experiences can have an impact on your brain. It becomes ultra-sensitive. Even the slightest thing can trigger fear-based thoughts and reactions.

The overthinking, the catastrophising, the anxiety all come from fear caused by past traumatic events, or so some experts say. I am not dismissing the raging hormones here that we have after childbirth, during our periods and during menopause. Overthinking and anxiety can be at their worst during these times. I know for a fact my Head Hooligan used to be out of control a lot when I was having a period. I am now perimenopausal, so there have been lots of times when I have thought I'm losing the plot.

What is your fear? What is your worst-case scenario? I hope you spot it in the next few paragraphs because once you realise what it is, life does become a tad easier (and I mean a tad).

You'll be surprised to learn (I was) that there are only five universal fears, according to Dr Karl Albrecht the author of *Brain Power and Social Intelligence, The New*

Science of Success.

These five fears are where almost all our other fears stem from and when we let go of the notion of fear as the monster inside us and actually see fear as information, we can think about them consciously and they become less scary, because fear of fear probably causes more problems in our lives than fear itself (I think President Roosevelt quoted similar once).

The universal trigger for fear is a threat to ourselves, whether it be emotional, physical or psychological and whether it be real or imagined.

Fear can take over as I've described in Chapter One. It can cause you to overthink and catastrophise and imagine every worst-case scenario that your poor Head Hooligan can conjure up, but it's not nearly as complicated as we try to make it.

A simple and useful definition of fear is 'an anxious feeling, caused by anticipationof some imagined event or experience' (I pinched that from Google). And, if you're like me, and you most probably are, we all know where that can lead!

The professionals would say that the anxious feelings we get when we're afraid is a biologically built-in reaction. Our reactions to fear give us the same feelings we get when we're afraid of getting bitten by a dog, getting dumped by your fella (or lady) or being diagnosed with an illness.

Fear, like all other emotions, is basically *information*. It offers us knowledge and understanding; if we choose to accept it.

We no longer need our primal fears, there are no sabre tooth tigers waiting to pounce on us and actually most of us sit in nice cozy warm houses with our cupboards full (well almost full). So, our brain has become all modern and created intellectual fears, and now instead we're fearing being scared of failing or getting stuck in a bloody lift. However I've listed the five basic fears by Dr Karl Albrecht below.

I have taken some of his words and mixed them with my own just to make it more relatable.

Extinction – The fear of 'just not being here', a fear of 'ceasing to exist'. This is a more fundamental way to express it than just having a fear of dying, because it hits you right in the heart. The thought of no longer 'being' can cause anxiety in most of us. Can you imagine your whole *you* just not being here? A very scary thought for the 'normal' human and an absolute nightmare of a thought for those who have experienced trauma in the past and overthink such things.

Mutilation – The fear of losing any part of our beautiful bodies. The idea of having our body's boundaries invaded, or of losing an organ, or natural function. This could be any fear where we would feel unsafe or under attack. Anxiety about animals such as bugs, spiders, snakes and other creepy things arises from fear of mutilation, as do crowds, needles and germs. I bet a lot of us went through some of these fears during the height of the COVID-19 pandemic, this and the fear of extinction, for sure.

Loss of Autonomy – As Dr Albrecht puts it: 'The fear of being immobilised, paralysed, restricted, enveloped, overwhelmed, entrapped, imprisoned, smothered, or otherwise controlled by circumstances beyond our control.' Our fear of being smothered, restricted, unable to take care of ourselves or being dependent on others can apply to situations in our lives – or our relationships. A trigger for this fear would be a controlling relationship, a debilitating illness, even you beautiful new mamas from time to time will feel this fear, due to feeling overwhelmed and restricted even trapped at times, because you can't give those babies up (I know you don't want to, but there are times we all want some let up).

Separation – Rejection – Abandonment. We girls have a strong need to belong. This is my biggest fear.

From being a little girl, I have actually feared upsetting people. It's not about them, it's about *me* being rejected or even abandoned. Dr Albrecht refers to this fear as 'loss of connectedness; of becoming a non-person – not wanted, respected, or valued by anyone else', which literally threatens our wellbeing and survival. This is where my irritating people-pleasing comes from, and the more I understand it the more I feel less inspired to do it.

Humiliation, Shame or Worthlessness. Dr Albrecht's description of this is ego-death. The fear of humiliation, shame or any other mechanism of profound self-disapproval that threatens the loss of oneself. The shattering loss of one's sense of lovability, capability and worthiness. From a spiritual aspect ego-death is loss of ego and return to love because actually when we lose the ego, we tend not to care what others think, so this one has a double meaning for me, depending on the source, i.e., spiritual or psychological. But nevertheless, it's one of the five universal fears. And I could be totally wrong but that's my view.

And basically, I think (me who's not qualified in psychology nor has a metaphysics degree) if you just think about the above things and rationalise them and your Head Hooligan doesn't take over, that's great. But, if you're like me, and these fears creep into your mind almost as though they have a mind of their own and your Head Hooligan won't let up thinking over them, then your life is running on a fear-based cycle.

Every one of you will worry about all of the above at some point. It's the overthinker, though, whose life is running on a fear-based cycle, which is no good for anybody who wants to live a fulfilling stress-free life of inner peace. In fact, even if you don't want a life of inner peace but want to understand how to stop that chitter-chatter, then you can learn how to do that.

The mental symptoms that can result from living in fear will send us overthinkers into a wild oscillation of the mind, which goes back and forth with its constant bloody whining. (I keep getting images as I write of my Head Hooligan spinning freely as she dictates her next fear-based thought.

If you experience any of the symptoms below, then it's possible you are living in fear.

Are you overly sensitive to criticism and do you find it hard to trust others?

There will be times you'll find it difficult to make new friends unless you can be sure that they like you (and let's face it, we never know what the other person is thinking) and you will take extreme measures to avoid rejection or separation. Or you will be full-on as you constantly want to please people and can't do enough for them very early on in the relationship, and this can come across as off-putting, even if you don't intend to be.

Looking back, have you created a pattern of unhealthy relationships? Do you get comments like: 'You can't half pick 'em!'? (By the way, if you do, tell the judgers to 'do one'!)

Do you constantly look outside yourself for cues on how to be; often questioning your sense of self or place in the world?

This is particularly apt for women. All too often, especially in today's world of social media, we compare our lives to those of others.

Do you feel a disconnect from who you've been and have no sense of who you will become next?

This can be distressing for the woman who just wants peace.

Do you experience a lack of drive or motivation?

Are you someone who feels constantly bored and always seems to drive on empty, like life has no meaning? Maybe you ask yourself, 'What is the point?'

There are those who scare themselves thinking about what will happen if they die, and worrying so much about it, and what will happen to their children or other loved ones, that it's overwhelming. Me and my Head Hooligan have been to far too many mental funerals and ended up sobbing with these thoughts.

Those who experience a lack of drive or motivation may feel unfulfilled in their relationships with others and could feel disaffected at home and at work and find themselves on the constant spiral of rumination on what is the point of life.

Are you worn out yet?

Living in a fear-based mind will wear you out, it will cause you pain that resides in your body and then your Head Hooligan starts with, 'I'm dying! I have a terminal illness!' and so it continues. But as you spiral out of control, remember, this negative overthinking is actually adding to the pain. It's like a vicious circle going round from your mind to your body.

And all the while you're wasting your precious time, life is passing you by.

The odd fact is, we are actually comforted by these thoughts and feelings. I've already touched on the fact that we actually become addicted to overthinking and creating our fear-based life.

You might have put the book down now because that sounds ludicrous.

If you haven't put the book down *thank you* because it's good to understand the following if you're wanting to ease off with internal nagging.

When you're in a state of fear, your fight or flight response kicks in (the brain remembering some type of danger so it's on high alert) and the hormones in your brain such as dopamine are released along with adrenaline, which for a minute can make us physically and emotionally charged, almost like a mini-high. And, like any mini-high, it's momentarily nice.

We don't want to overthink, (well I certainly don't), we don't want to feel negative, and we don't want to feel anxious, but because when we *are* anxious, we think and catastrophise and make up stories in our heads and we find ourselves in that vicious cycle, we end up overthinking. It's very complex and very circular. There are other reasons for this which I'll cover later.

Also, there is a familiarity around going in our thoughts and having the anxiety that goes with them, we're used to that feeling, horrendous as it is, it is familiar and subconsciously you will find comfort! Remember the times you've gone to someone you're familiar with as opposed to actually liking them, but because there is no one else available, they're better than nothing? That is what you're doing. You're settling with these thoughts because they're better than nothing... or are they? And why not change the thoughts so they aren't so damaging?

There *is* a way to calm these thoughts. Some people have even learnt to have constant inner peace. But we're on baby steps here, you're not going to put this book down and be in a state of inner bliss; although if I had one wish, I would send that to all the girls who are struggling and reading this.

I have taught myself how to get close to inner peace. I'm not fully there yet and I don't live in a state of inner peace all the time, but more often now 'it' visits me during my overthinking attacks. I welcome it massively and I have that inner peace feeling several times a day now.

It was actually hard work at first and even quite scary to not actually *worry*. Initially I used to think, '*Oh... I'm not worrying... nothing's wrong...*' and I'd try and find something wrong to worry about!

Marianne was spot on with her quote.

"Our deepest fear is that we are powerful beyond measure. It is our light, not our darkness that most frightens us." – Marianne Williamson

Chapter Three - Her Trauma and Post Traumatic Stress Disorder (PTSD)

Trauma is an emotional response to a dreadful event that has happened, events such as an accident, abuse, rape or a natural disaster. Immediately after the event we can feel shocked and distraught. These feelings can have a long-term effect on you, such as bad dreams, panic attacks and even flashbacks, and in turn, can impact your relationship with others. It can affect you physically too, by way of headaches and sick feelings. Depending on your perception of trauma, a trauma can lead to you having feelings of helplessness and wide open to mental health problems and can cause Post Traumatic Stress Disorder (PTSD).

There are different types of trauma, but for the sake of making this easy to understand and uncomplicated (because I don't want you to have to think too much and I want you to just have an easy read), I'm generalising in saying that trauma leads to PTSD.

It actually depends on the person's perception, not all things affect us in the same way.

I started laughing when my GP diagnosed me with PTSD seven years ago. I even asked him if he was joking and explained that although my situation had been bad, I hadn't been to war and witnessed my mates being blown to shreds and come home with half of my face hanging off.

He explained that whilst you're in a traumatic situation, i.e., something that is horrifying to you, or a situation where you are totally helpless, you're constantly in that flight, freeze or fight response (your body's reaction to a stressful or frightening situation; do I run, do I freeze, or do I stay and fight?). It's in the aftermath that your brain goes: 'What the actual fuck just happened to me?' (My doctor didn't say fuck, by the way, this is just my non-classy interpretation.)

He said, 'Your poor head doesn't know whether to fight, freeze or flight now, so it's become over sensitive and thinks you're in constant danger and are unsafe.'

For too many years I had been in a bad relationship. It was coercive, controlling, abusive both physically and mentally. It had ended when things had gone too far, and I finally phoned the police and was finally rid of that part of my life.

Or so I thought. Because although the bad treatment had disappeared, the residual mess that my Head Hooligan turned into became worse than ever.

There was a court case at which they were found 'not guilty', of course, because the law doesn't understand coercive control, nor does it understand the behaviour of and how these abusers work.

They say they do, but they don't. The lack of knowledge and education in this field is backwards and I'm sorry for using such an awful word, but we might as well still be in Tudor times. There are so many women (I'm going to swear again) in this fucking situation, it's horrifying.

Just last night I joined a private Facebook Page to do a walkathon for Refuge, a charity for women and children against domestic violence. The page was created so that the members could hook up with other walkers, share stories and relate to and egg each other on.

I read so many women's posts.

They are asked to put 'TRIGGER' as the heading of their post because the charity is aware of how sensitive the rest of the women readers will be. The stories made me cry as did the sheer bravery of the women. The heading was right. It was a massive trigger for me.

I used to be in another group for survivors of domestic abuse, again another site where women could connect and share their stories. These were horrific to read to the point I had to leave. It wasn't helpful for me, albeit helpful for many others.

Their stories of how they were living in fear, hour by hour, how they were so frightened that they would be killed, along with their children, were terrifying to read.

These women are too scared to leave, so are getting hurt and humiliated every day.

One of the women even had her children taken away from her because her abuser husband worked as a solicitor and knew every rule in the book; absolutely terrifying for the helpless girl and her babies.

Women are still being made to do things against their will and can see no way out.

Alternatively, if they've managed to get out, they may still be stalked and harassed, followed and mentally tormented online.

Yes, online. Unfortunately, in this day and age you don't have to be face-to-face with someone to be bullied. The modern world of social media is the perfect platform from which bullies thrive. It's so much easier for these cowards to abuse and bully women online as they hide behind their keyboards. 'Go, *men!*' Did I just use the word men? Not into man-bashing, but these 'type' of men are extremely damaging.

It makes me worry for our young girls growing up in this very exposing world of social media. You can't piss without someone snapping you, for your picture to be then to be uploaded on Facebook, Instagram, TikTok... and whatever other source of bollocks our kids are growing up around.

I can't imagine back in the 80s, my first boyfriend, after dumping me, being photographed with his tongue in the ear of some beautiful girl who has legs to die for.

These young girls are tormented daily with these types of images flooding their timelines and then there is the intimidation that goes on.

But having friends with teenage girls, the stories I hear are heart-breaking.

Such as a group of gorgeous young girlies, all photographed out together having fun, whilst the young girl who has been left out is sitting on her bed watching her so-called friends having a good time without her, on her timeline.

When she looks later, she is blocked. All the while she's juggling convincing Mum that she's OK and that nothing is bothering her and at the same time trying to figure out what she's done wrong. The shame is too much at this point for a young girl, so she's using her mask early-doors. Worse still, how will she face them all at school on Monday?

If she experiences this behaviour repeatedly, which may not seem anywhere near as dramatic as war (which we often relate to PTSD), it's the sort of stuff that leads to fear of abandonment and can be so damaging in years to come. This is the stuff trauma is made from and can eventually lead to PTSD.

It was only from my conversation with my GP that has made me realise just how many different scenarios can cause PTSD like this.

All teenagers have to go through various challenges, not all with have PTSD, but for some they will. Who is to blame? Parents? Social media? Finding blame is not important, blaming just holds us back.

I personally truly believe that by blaming parents, or others for our lives, it holds us back. Instead, *we* have to be responsible for ourselves, if we stop attributing blame, it frees us to just get on. By always blaming, it's suggesting we can't do anything about it. Although blaming our parents can seem the obvious thing to do, don't. Stop now. I'm not saying become your mother's best friend if you have a difficult relationship, but what I am saying is stop blaming your past or her words. Instead, allow yourself to be free from that blame. Y*ou* are responsible for how you live the rest of your life. If your Head Hooligan begins quoting your mother's unkind phrases, tell it to be quiet. Don't listen to it. You don't need to listen to it. You listen to what you want. You are in control, you're an adult. You can do this.

Back to the bullies, there is always something deeper

going on with a bully, we've always been told this. A usual response from grown-ups was telling us that the bullies were just jealous.

It's deeper than that; they're just living in self-perpetuating fear (doesn't help though when you're on the receiving end; being bullied).

A lot of shame is developed in our teenage years due to the environment around us, growing up at home – easy for some of you, not so easy for others. As you develop boobs and get your periods, which as we all know throw you mentally and physically until your 50s (but that's another story!) every month for some of us can be a week of hell.

School – with the challenge of trying to fit in everyday, faced with the bullying (and not everyone experiences it, I know). I was called goofy (because my teeth stuck out) straight away in my teenage years. I was made to feel ugly. I remember always trying to have the perfect hair and the right clothes, which was difficult given my upbringing. I would always try to fit in, and, because of this, my people-pleasing came out the most in that period of my life.

I remember *our* school bully used to scratch your hands with her thick horrible nails, her objective was to draw blood. I'll never forget watching her doing it to others, whilst being thankful that it wasn't me but horrified for the poor girl whose hand was bleeding.

When the environment around you is toxic, you will take it with you for years, these incidents showing up as trauma later in life. You might have forgotten all about it, until something triggers you and it's right back with you, another contributing factor to PTSD.

Anyway, back to me!

My GP diagnosing me with PTSD made me think about the court case and recognise what it made me feel.

It was horrendous. I have never felt so afraid and sickened in my whole life. I was having to face my abuser in court. Luckily for me there was a protection shield between us, but I could hear them and that was enough. There is a new process now that the courts have delivered where you can actually record your witness statement. It's a little further on in protecting witnesses, but it mustn't have been around then, or I would have requested it.

The solicitor (who was provided by the court) representing me kept flitting in and out of the witness protection suite as though checking on a small child. She barely said two words, never mind listen to my side of the story. The lady from the Domestic Violence (DV) team who worked with the police had three appointments at the same time as mine, so other than making me a brew, her input was minimal and, bless her, that was due to the lack of resources against the volume of women that needed them.

The wasted ordeal and hearing those words 'not guilty' added to my stress and anxiety; they didn't believe me. Maybe I had got it wrong. Because they didn't believe me, she started, and I had absolutely no room for her – my Head Hooligan. *'It's because you didn't get your story right, it's because they thought you were lying, it's because you came across like a bloody idiot.'*

And my abuser was free to go with no restraining order, nothing.

I have to add here that even though I have just documented an ordeal which felt wasted; *it wasn't wasted,* but it took me years to get to that stage in my head. And although I said that many women leaving an abusive relationship still may have their abuser following them, it's important they take the steps of getting out, of putting a stop to it, in a safe way. It may feel difficult or impossible, but you *can* do it.

I know now, after taming my Head Hooligan, that it was so brave of me (thanks, Head Hooligan, you do come up trumps now).

'You did it, babe,' she croons now.

'You stopped the bullying.

You showed the world that you would not *be messed about with.*

You are so brave.

You are so clever.'

She's right, and I'd do it again and again if, God forbid, I had to.

I would also encourage you, if you're in that situation, to see it through as difficult as it is.

But at the time, the whole experience left me living in fear more times than I care to think about.

It was during that period – just after the court case – that my Head Hooligan seemed to move into my head permanently. She was like a squatter. She became louder than ever because she was there to stay, and at this time of my life, I had no idea how to get rid of my negative, intrusive thoughts.

Once my GP said I had PTSD, I understood why. I just wasn't sure what to do with it all and what it meant. I looked back at how I felt on the lead up to the court case.

I would dwell on the relationship night after night.

My Head Hooligan would sit in my head ready to judge and berate me.

'How could you let that happen to you?

You put other people in danger!

Your grown-up children must think you're an idiot!

You could have been seriously hurt or killed!

What were you thinking, allowing that?

Why weren't you stronger? You're so weak and gullible at times!

Why didn't you listen to me and do it sooner?

You're an idiot. You must be thick; something is wrong with you!'

And, looking back, I could see what I did. I picked up where my abuser left off and continued being abused by *myself*.

When I studied PTSD, I knew the doctor was right; I *do* have PTSD.

But it wasn't as easy as going to the GP and getting a diagnosis. It took a big moment for me to get to the GP in the first place.

Months after the relationship but before the court case, I checked that my doors were locked every minute of the day.

But nights were the worst.

I'd check under my bed several times during the night. I'd sit up in bed all night afraid to sleep. No windows were ever left open.

This fear was formed in my formative years, I was

always scared of the dark as a little girl, so it makes sense that dark nights in an anxious state would affect me after experiencing such trauma.

Trauma is your own perception, and no one can tell you any differently.

But that fearful child was back, with a whole lot more to deal with than just the dark nights.

Then it came, the moment which led to me recognising that I had to go and see my GP. I got a phone call that my older son (who had been staying with me for protection) was in a horrific car crash and how he got out alive we will never know. He spent three weeks in intensive care. I didn't know whether he would live or die. The fear was gripping me, and I didn't know if I could take anymore.

In this scenario, funnily enough, my Head Hooligan was kind to me more than she was mean, although she did have the odd jibe.

'He will be OK, you know.

He's young and strong.'

Then:

'But people do lose their kids, why are you so different?

What will you do if he never walks again?'

But we bloody well carry on. We are definitely, as human beings, hard-wired to survive, because at that point of my life, if a big alien ship would have landed on our road and said, 'Come!' I'd have been off like a shot.

Not only was I gripped with fear of losing my son, but I was also now alone in the house with my younger son, who at the time was a child.

I felt like I had treacle on the soles of my feet. I wasn't sleeping a wink. I was scared and knackered, but I had to go to the hospital daily and I had to look after my younger son, and I had to work, or I wouldn't be able to put petrol in my car to get to the hospital. I was exhausted.

Once my son started to recover and I knew he was going to be OK... it started to manifest itself even more.

I became hypersensitive. I later learnt this is a natural part of PTSD.

I remember my first panic attack. I was lying in bed one night and my older son was downstairs, playing on the PlayStation, he clumsily kept dropping the controller onto the wooden floor (yep, fully recovered and back to driving me mad).

Every time I heard the thud of it falling on the floor, I got an electric shock feeling in my head and my stomach felt sick.

It was a massive trigger for me. My heart was pounding through my chest as I remembered what the abuser's reaction would have been to that noise and my son still being awake.

I felt the fear in my stomach, as it tied itself in knots. I was confused, though, because realistically my son could drop the remote a hundred times and it wouldn't matter a jot. The abuser wasn't in our lives anymore. I lay there and actually smiled as I thought, 'It's OK now, it's really OK.' But he dropped it again.

My arms went numb and started tingling. I felt like I was having an out-of-body experience as the room became dreamlike. I couldn't breathe.

I panted and tried to fight against the feeling, but it was getting worse and worse. I sat up in bed in sheer panic and waited for it to subside. As I did, my son popped in my bedroom to check I was OK. I remember nodding my head as I didn't want him to know what was happening.

The nightmares had begun. Flashbacks began hitting me in the face every day.

I found myself constantly shaking my head as if to refuse to let it all back in, but it never worked. I didn't like it and I needed to understand what was happening to me. I knew I had to get help; I felt like I was losing my mind. I needed help, I knew it, and this event with the remote-control dropping was the catalyst for me making the appointment.

I suppose the realisation of the trigger made it clear

to me. I probably didn't realise it at the time, but it was the beginning of my healing journey. I realised I needed help; I recognised my symptoms were something I'd not experienced before.

Trauma is a word that can mean so much but is defined as 'a normal reaction to an abnormal event'. The effect of a traumatic incident can affect us in many different ways and leave us reeling for years, if untreated.

To qualify as a contributing event to PTSD the traumatic event must be 'an event outside the range of a normal human experience', which does sound a bit dramatic because everything that happens to us could be in that range... but actually, it isn't, if you think about it. Being abused shouldn't be a normal human experience. PTSD is around perception for the individual. Depending on our past experiences, our perceptions will be different. Therefore, what one person may see as a traumatic event, others may not.

So, don't let someone tell you otherwise; only you know what's happened to you and only you know how you're affected and the response your mind is having.

There are so many causes of trauma that happen in our formative years. The time between being a baby and an eight-year-old is when we learn quicker than any other stage of our lives, this is when we experience rapid cognitive (intellectual), social, emotional and physical development. These are the years when our minds need protecting the most, if you like, but life isn't that simple, is it?

So many events can lead to a child having their wellbeing rocked by trauma later on in life. If left unaddressed the following events can create issues in later life, particularly around mental and physical health:

An Accident

Chaos in a dysfunctional household

Death of a loved one

Emotional abuse or neglect

Physical abuse

Separation from a parent

Stress caused by poverty

Sexual abuse

Violence

War

An experience, or repeated experiences, may leave a child with an overwhelming sense of fear and loss, making them feel that they have no safety or control over their little lives. For some children these feelings become so intense that they get in the way of their continued physical, emotional, social or intellectual development.

This is childhood trauma.

Remember back in the day none of this would have been recognised. We were told to, 'Get on with it!' or 'Don't be soft!' Hopefully there is a lot more support for the kids of today.

So, once I realised that I had PTSD and that I was living in hypersensitive mode, I needed to get better. But how can we get better from PTSD? By the way I'm not diagnosing you here, I'm merely making you aware that your overthinking, stress and anxieties could, and possibly do, come from trauma, either recognised or unrecognised.

PTSD can be successfully treated, even when it develops many years after the traumatic event. Of course, treatment will depend on the severity of the symptoms and how soon they occur after the traumatic event.

If you're recognising yourself in my words, please go and see your GP and explain what's going on, you can self-refer or be referred for counselling or other psychological therapies.

It's a great start if you recognise, you're struggling to ask for help. Such a brave thing to do and it's better, so much better, than trying to plod on with treacle on your feet and a Head Hooligan with treacle on her feet too.

If you don't feel like you're ready to talk now, that's

OK too. A good idea is to monitor your symptoms to see whether or not they improve or get worse without treatment. Maybe make a note of how you're feeling and what is triggering you.

If you start to feel like you're on high alert all the time or getting flashbacks, then it's definitely time to seek help.

When you suddenly start to feel shit, try and work out what the trigger is.

Medication. There, I said it. There is still a stigma around taking medication to help mental health symptoms. I don't care what anybody says, (I can say this now as I'm not so much of a people-pleaser anymore!) this is your choice, your mind, your thoughts. And if medication can help that then why not?

I once knew a girl who was going through an adoption process but because she had taken antidepressants in the past, she was refused the child on the account that she might become unstable again.

So, it can be off-putting when you're receiving feedback like that.

What a bad mother she would have made for taking medication to make herself better (I am being sarcastic, obviously) because, if you had asthma, you'd use an inhaler, just as if you had a cut on your finger, you'd put a plaster on it.

Forget the stigma, it's ridiculous. Medication is there to make you better. We are so lucky to have that choice too and that's what it has to be, a choice. *Your choice*.

Paroxetine and mirtazapine are designed to help you with response rates (I think that might mean how you react to triggers), but it is also said they can help you with sleep disturbance and they reduce each symptom cluster of PTSD.

I was given paroxetine when I was diagnosed, it helped at the time and I'm glad I took them.

I did also want to heal in a more holistic way; both ways help. A counsellor once said to me, 'The medication is your plaster, but the real fix is to address the thoughts in your head.'

There are therapies such as Trauma-Focused Cognitive Behavioural Therapy (TF-CBT) or Eye Movement Desensitisation and Reprocessing (EMDR).

I'll keep reminding you at points when I start waffling on that I'm not a doctor and can't diagnose anything. I can, however, give advice on treatment if you *are* diagnosed.

As trauma affects the brain, it does become slightly damaged (although the brain is so resilient it can fix itself) because it experiences excessive activation in certain areas related to fear. It's like an alarm going off that knows from memory that something bad is going to happen.

Well, when you've suffered trauma, it's like the bell that constantly dings on a hotel desk and unfortunately you get to a point where you always feel like something is wrong or something bad is going to happen.

Of course, all this is happening in the background, subconsciously. You're unaware what is going on and why, it all just happens, making you feel shit most of the time.

I fully recognise now that my panic attack was triggered by the sound of my son dropping the remote control, which triggered my brain to react in a way that it remembered from the past. So, although at the time I was at a very low point, it *was* the start of my healing. What's that saying? If you reach rock bottom, there's only one way to go and that is up.

Being aware will totally help you deal with most of the feelings, most of the time.

So, for example, I would text someone and if they didn't reply instantly I would get anxious. My Head Hooligan used to kick in and I'd start to think all sorts *again*. You must know the script by now?

Off she'd go:

'What have you done wrong?

In what way have you offended them?

Because you will have done.

They don't like you!

There's going to be an argument, they've fallen out with you!'

Don't worry I actually used to bore myself at times, but what I'm saying is – before, a simple incident like this could send me reeling for hours, but *now* I deal with it differently. I make my Head Hooligan into my Head Buddy and have her talk to me in a nicer way, or I distract myself and get on with something else.

Another way I deal with instances like this is by becoming aware! I'm aware that because I have PTSD the little bit in my brain isn't working properly, so it may be telling me I am in danger (as I often was) or something is wrong, (as it often was) and it wants me to get ready to fight or flight (as it used to often). I am on hyper alert and hypersensitive to anything that I think represents danger, but I know it now. I tell myself I am no longer in danger.

I am also very aware that because this is happening in my brain, the feelings of deep anxiety that I have aren't real. Because, in reality, I am safe, and nothing is wrong and nothing *bad* will happen from lying there overthinking. But if it does, I've had more than enough bloody practice to deal with such things. So, I observe that feeling now, just observe it and acknowledge it. Winking at my Head Hooligan as I take back the control. She stays quiet as I don't react to it, I don't try and fight it anymore, as doing so will make me feel even worse and it's not *real*, I have nothing to fear. If she tries it now, I make her say things differently to me.

'Well, you've done nothing wrong.

She could be busy.

You've not offended them intentionally.

They do like you.

Nothing is wrong you'll see.'

I am aware that bad things *do* happen, but the bad things that do happen don't come out of my head. My head never creates the bad, it's just me catastrophising, which is natural for someone struggling with PTSD.

Once I am aware, I step into the moment, *right into the moment,* and take in what is going on around me. I take a great big sigh, as this resets my nervous system, then I steady my breathing and listen to it as I do so. Sometimes I breathe in and count to four, hold my breath and count to four and breathe out for seven seconds. It just stops my thoughts of panic for a while whilst I count and breathe calmly. Remember you can't overthink and do something else at the same time.

That stops Head Hooligan dead in her tracks and calms the little bit in my brain that isn't working properly. I will start to feel some headspace. I even say out loud sometimes,

'It's OK, I'm safe.' In doing this I'm actually re-training the little bit in my brain that's on hyper alert constantly. It will start to realise that I'm no longer in danger. If you say something positive often enough your subconscious will pick it up and it will become re-programmed to accept it as a fact, a belief.

I sometimes sit in the garden and look at every leaf I can see on a tree, or I listen to every bird I can hear. I concentrate hard on every flower I can see, and I inhale and enjoy whatever weather I'm lucky enough to experience.

In bed I will listen carefully to my breathing, paying it full attention. Don't get me wrong, my mind wanders back to my thoughts; I wouldn't be alive if I didn't have thoughts. When they come back into my head again, I acknowledge my little Head Hooligan and I observe the thought as though I'm looking down on it, just observing, with no reaction to it. It's so hard to do at times but remember how bloody strong you are. Now, I go right back to my breathing. I will also do a body scan and focus on every inch of my body, paying attention to how it feels and whether or not I can feel any tension in any particular areas.

When I am aware and, in the moment, my Head Hooligan can't get in, she's probably floating on a cloud having a rest somewhere.

I am aware that the more I do this the less I overthink and catastrophise.

Now I am aware of what I need to do to get over the attacks that have debilitated my poor gorgeous head in the past.

Let's be honest, in all of this I want to live, and I know you do too as you've made it this far.

Do you want to live in constant fear all the time? Let me tell you this for nothing, when you're on your deathbed, you'll wonder what the hell you were thinking, and you will want to go back and do it all again, but this time you will pay attention.

So, yes, I have PTSD, and yes, it causes me to overthink and catastrophise, but I will stand tall as I battle it out to have my peaceful inner self show up. And, if I'm honest, as the years have gone on, and because I've worked so hard on it, it really has become easier and easier.

There are no truer words said than the quote below.

"Worrying does not take away tomorrow's troubles. It takes away today's peace."

Randy Armstrong

Chapter Four - Lady Empaths

Another part of me learning more about myself and gaining freedom was having to accept some terminologies applied to me. One of which was an empath. I'd never heard of it before, and when an old friend of mine mentioned she thought I was an empath, she explained that it made me attractive to the narcissist type, because they see someone who will fulfil their need in the most selfless way.

I was almost offended and saw it as a bad thing, and of course started to overthink. As my Head Hooligan sat there, this time on her chaise lounge, eating grapes, she taunted, *'It's because you're a mug!'*

Because my friend had tied being an empath in with narcissism, I thought it was a bad thing, but I started to wonder how can having empathy be a *bad* thing? But she'd got me curious and my Head Hooligan, turned on her front now on the chaise longue, stated, *'You need to sort this or be a mug forever. What else do your friends think about you?'*

Eventually I decided to look into it, and the more I read, the more I realised my friend was right – I am an empath. But because I understand it better and I'm aware, I embrace it and have learnt how to not allow my empath self to be drained of too much energy. I can hear you demanding now, what *is* an empath? Or maybe you already know and you're wondering how I've learnt to embrace being one? Well... here goes...

If you've ever felt such an awareness of other people's emotions or are really attuned to someone else's feelings, there is a chance that you are an empath. If you can literally *feel* how someone else is feeling at a deep emotional level, then you're definitely an empath.

An empath can literally feel the energy of those around them – good or bad – but more often than not it's the bad energy that they take on for themselves.

Empathy is the ability to feel for someone else's experiences outside your own perspective. For example, a friend loses her cat. You don't even have a cat, have never had a cat, yet you can understand her level of pain.

Empaths are slightly different as they take it one step further, they will actually feel the pain and sadness for their friend losing the cat as though it's their own experience.

Taking on other people's energy is absolutely draining; this leaves the empath in total confusion as to whose energy is whose. God help you if you're an empath with anxiety or a sensitive empath, which you possibly could be.

I remember interviewing a man once for a job, he was answering the questions as he should have been doing, but I could feel sadness from him, it was right in the pit of my stomach and I wanted to get up, go around to the other side of the table and give him a big hug.

After he got the job, he later told me that his wife had not long died and that he needed the job to look after his son. I was devastated for days, but I'd felt it too. I'd felt it when I was with him. I'm so glad we employed him.

An empath doesn't just feel for someone they feel *with* someone; they're extremely sensitive to other people's feelings and can usually tell straight away by just looking at someone's face what their mood is or how they are feeling. Being sensitive isn't a weakness, by the way. I'm saying this because I've been called 'too sensitive' so many times and usually in a chastising way, when actually I just pick up on how people are feeling or instantly know when someone is unhappy with me.

It's not great being an empath, coupled with being a people-pleaser; it can be bloody hard work. As if we've not got enough on without taking on someone else's emotions. Suffering from anxiety does not help you when you're an empath, it only adds to the stress that you're already in the midst of.

If you are an empath, although you will be a good listener and you will always find that your friends and family come to you first with their problems, because of your caring nature, you will also find that these same people will take advantage of your good nature and your kindness and be a constant drain on your energy.

Also, if you're an empath, you will dread conflict and will do anything to keep the peace. Arguments and fights will cause you massive distress because not only are you dealing with your own feelings, but you're also trying to deal with everyone else's feelings around you; again, this can become absolutely exhausting. And this is also why we often say yes when we really should be saying no, and we quite often put other people's feelings and needs before our own. But why? Why shouldn't *we* come first? First of all, if we're not mentally healthy, not only do we suffer but our work suffers, our family suffers. When you get on a flight, the flight attendant always tells you to put your own oxygen mask on first before helping others. It's the same concept with being an empath, you're no good to anyone unless you're well.

Recognise yourself?

There are some benefits to being an empath, however, so don't write it off just yet, for it does have its uses. If someone is feeling sad or depressed and they haven't yet opened up, you will know because you'll pick it up from them. It's a good skill to have, for once you've gained that person's trust, you're in a good position to help. As I said before – you will be a good listener, you're caring, and some of you are also good healers.

Now, that's all well and good if you're in a strong place yourself, but given you've picked up this book, the probability is you're not in a good place and you're an overthinking wreck, like I was. So, my advice in this instance would be to take care of you, until you're ready to take on the stress of others.

Most importantly, if you're an empath, stay away from the toxic, abusive people. This isn't a good match because as you take on their low moods, their negative emotions will become your own.

Abusive and toxic people will play on the empath's good nature and absolutely tie them in knots.

Unfortunately, girlies, we are more likely to be empaths than our male counterparts because, as we know, they just don't have that depth of feeling about certain things, never mind feeling someone else's emotions.

People ask – is an empath a narcissist? The answer is, no, they are total opposites. The narcissist trait is in us all, but there is a spectrum and different levels. It starts with traits, right through to a Narcissist Personality Disorder (NPD) The narcissist feels no empathy and their main goal is to feel admired. Whereas an empath is highly sensitive and in tune with other people's emotions.

When the two meet, the narcissist will keep the empath in a cycle of abuse and will use them as the scapegoat for their own dysfunctional feelings, whilst the empath will internalise their feelings and accept all the blame, they throw at them.

All genders can be narcissists, this is not specific to men at all, a lot of people I know have grown up with a narcissist mother, who has left them reeling in their adult life.

There is a definite mismatch between an empath and a narcissist, as the narcissist throws their tantrums, all the empath will do is want them to feel OK. She will do absolutely anything to help, even accepting all the blame for the narcissist's poor behaviour, empathising all the while feeling their torment and taking on the need to please and fix them, whilst wrapped up in their toxic behaviour, breathing in their energy like a stale poison that will eventually hit her physically and mentally. It's a total headfuck; as her empathetic nature will ensure that her obsession with wanting to please and make it right, will keep her going in her flight and fight responses, hooking the narcissist in on their need for power journey.

A narcissist rarely feels OK, their energy is often bad, creating an unsettled environment for the empath. The narcissist will constantly play the empath, picking up on their weaknesses, keeping them in this state as part of the control that they demand. They will gaslight and use vile words against the empath, so that she's constantly on her toes. They will say things like 'I know my ex was better at that, but that was because she cared more' so that the empath will then absolutely do the best she can to be better than the ex. Or if you try to defend yourself or say you didn't like something, they then pick up on the vulnerability. 'You are so anxious, why would you think I meant it like that? Honestly, you should see the doctor, you let your emotions get away with you!'

So, feeling sad and taking on their pain, she will still try and be the best she can be for them both. Can you feel the turmoil between the narcissist and the empath? It's an absolute lethal combination and one to be avoided.

However, the narcissist will always prey on an empath as it's a dead cert that they hit the jackpot.

I am no way blaming an empath in this, abuse is abuse and whoever is the perpetrator and causes mental and physical harm to another, is in the wrong.

The narcissist will always say it's the other person, regardless as to whether they are an empath or not, who is at fault and it's the empath who is the abuser.

This is another example of gaslighting. It's a very confusing situation and one that will leave you scarred for years later. If you're in a situation that feels as toxic as I've described above, everyone else would tell you to get out. But that's easier said than done, especially when the empath is in a state of fear and confusion. I want to say, please stay safe and get help and advice. There *is* life after abuse; for that I promise. I know you're scared; I know you're confused, but please tell someone *now*.

Because empaths are so sensitive, the probability that they will experience some levels of post-traumatic stress is high. The relationship with a narcissist is definitely one of them, but you will have always been an empath, so for years you will have been on sensory overload and will have had more than your fair share of adrenaline rushes. This could also stem from early neglect, abuse or even having a constant feeling of 'not being seen' and the little empath not being supported with her emotions.

There are many reasons why an empath can perceive trauma, some of them are... If your parents argued often; imagine a little empathic girl trying to take on all those flying emotions and how confusing it would have been. If your siblings were always at loggerheads. If you were yelled at repeatedly as a child. If you were physically abused, or emotionally abused. If you were shamed into being 'too sensitive'. If you were bullied.

There is hope out there. An *empowered* empath is one

of the strongest ladies you will know, she is in control, she is grounded, and she is bloody Superwoman.

Below are some strategies for the empath.

Set Clear Boundaries

It's hard to keep your own emotions in check and difficult to set boundaries as an empath.

Remember – no is a one-word sentence.

This is the hardest thing for an empath to do. When she says 'no', she feels that she is hurting the other person and starts to feel that pain. Then there is that need to not let anyone down, it's almost faulty wiring.

What will it really lead to if you say 'no'? You won't be any less thought of, and you need to protect yourself because you're no good to anybody if you're absolutely drained and exhausted, struggling with anxiety and overthinking it all.

If you're recognising yourself, I bet you have said no in the past and then gone over it a thousand times, questioning yourself about whether it was OK to do so. Are you OK with that? Are you my friend? Do you think I'm hopeless? Have I let you down?

STOP – no is no. It's up to 'them' what they think about you, and *we* can't control our own thoughts here, never mind everyone else's.

Another way to set your boundaries could be to arrange a set time that suits you *both*, for that needy friend and yourself, but you must be clear that you can't offer more than that. Be firm, be kind and you will feel better for it. You're still helping her, but on your terms. Remember a person who doesn't respect your boundaries isn't even your friend.

Protect Your Energy

Because an empath picks up on everyone else's energy no matter what the situation, it's challenging for her to not confuse her energy with another's. So, it's very important to protect your energy. You can do this by staying grounded. When grounded you are in control of your emotions and thoughts, and you accept all that is happening. You are in the moment.

Try staying focused on the present. Remain strong in your own self-worth. Remember you do have a purpose. Trust yourself. Stay connected to nature. Mediate. Breathe. Be mindful.

Become aware of the energy you're picking up. I now ask myself if this is my energy or someone else's, and once I realise it's someone else's, I let go of their feelings. My journaling helped with this. I started to understand the different energies invading my body and how to cope better by remembering they're *not me*. Journaling is great and it helps you notice if there's a pattern to when you find yourself taking on feelings of others.

Now I recognise how other people's energy can affect me *before* I go to any event or a meeting. I ground myself and ensure that I am always in the present moment, this helps me to stay strong and to not cave into any negative energy others have.

> "*I am solely responsible for my own joy, happiness and freedom.*"
>
> *Adele*

.

Chapter Five - Why She Triggers

It's possible you were triggered reading the last chapter, you might have felt really emotional reading the empath versus narcissist bit. It could have possibly taken you to a bad place in your memories and it might have left you feeling a bit sick.

You might be wondering why that feeling happened after reading the above.

I hope it didn't trigger you enough to put the book down, as this chapter might answer some questions as to why you feel like that when you read, hear or smell certain things. Stay calm, go with this one now, but only if you can.

A trigger is a stimulus in the brain that will prompt an involuntary recall of an experience, for example a certain smell or a piece of clothing. If they're a reminder of a traumatic experience, the trigger can cause you to remember the negative emotions you had at that time and it will replay them for you, causing you to sometimes feel like you're re-living the whole experience again. These feelings can erupt very quickly depending on your state of mind.

Triggers are not helpful for your mental health, and they often bring on symptoms or worsen them. It's better to avoid any scenario that could trigger you, but this isn't always possible.

When I lost my dad, I watched him being taken in an ambulance and we followed the blue lights to the hospital. The next few days were the worst of my life and I'm not sure anything will surpass it. The sickness and fear I felt was like nothing I'd ever experienced. When the doctor told me he was dying, I grabbed his shirt and begged him to save him.

It's actually amazing that we *do* deal with our fears internally, the mind is unbelievable because there are times, we have all thought that we can't take anymore, but we do. Women are so strong, so bloody strong, for what they go through and deal with.

Anyway, for ages afterwards, when I heard sirens or saw blue lights, my heart would skip a beat, I would feel that same feeling that I'd felt when the doctors said my dad was going to die. The pit of my stomach would tighten, vomit would form in my throat and my tears would flow *again*.

This is a trigger. The part of my brain that remembered the doctor telling me that my dad was going to die said to the part of my brain that triggers my flight or fight stimulus, 'There you go, love, remember that!' and my emotions were nudged. The memory of that awful day was, for a few minutes, real again. That's an unavoidable trigger because unfortunately ambulances fly past us all the time and there's nothing, I can do about that.

One thing I now do is avoid watching A&E programmes on TV because I know it will trigger me. Once you understand your own triggers, there is an element of controlling them.

I think many of you will relate to my next trigger. It was a daily trigger for me. Every day I was full of anxiety and panic and I had fear running through my veins.

The five universal fears were queuing up knocking on my head to go in, and my Head Hooligan was dressed up as an usher, standing there tall, greeting them.

It was when Boris Johnson announced that we all had to go into Lockdown in March 2020.

How did that make you feel, hearing those words?

You've already read that I had once been in a controlling relationship, so when the Prime Minister announced lockdown on the news, I felt like I heard the bars slamming against the walls and windows of my house. There was a massive cage around me that I couldn't get out of… *again.*

I still can't believe we were locked down in our homes for almost two years.

The mental health clean-up from that, even now, will be astronomical, but there will be very few resources available and, even though it's focused on this and there is help, it always seems to take a back seat.

During the time these decisions were being made I think mental health, amongst other things, was at the bottom of the list. But this virus didn't come with a book – it just ripped freely through the world without any knowing (and I guess lots of you have your opinions on the how). Whatever the cause, reason or how it started, it caused so much pain and grief it was untrue.

The fear of loss of autonomy smacked me right in the bastard face.

The loss of performing daily tasks outside the house, the fear of being immobilised, trapped and paralysed; and the fear of losing control – which we did, we all did in some way. It absolutely floored me on the inside, of course, because on the outside I had to get my son accustomed to our new home with my new partner. One minute we were excited about the prospect and then all of a sudden, we were trapped under the same roof, and they had hardly gotten to know each other.

It was a big deal for us all, mainly because of what my son and I had experienced previously. So, here I was fighting another virus, only this one was outside my home and not living with me, thank God. For here I was being controlled yet again, in a totally different way, but the trigger was huge.

I started to feel distraught when I'd watch the news; the stories told us that domestic violence figures had gone through the roof, and I felt it. The pain was almost unbearable. I could imagine what every woman in that situation was going through, locked down with an abuser.

My Head Hooligan had been a Head Buddy for a while, but I welcomed her back in a Head Hooligan role and we battled off scenarios to one another of what the women would be going through. I genuinely found it difficult to get it out of my head.

It would be *her* fault; the world was on lockdown. What would happen to her if she contracted Covid? The frustrated abuser would need an outlet because the 'controller' was getting a taste of their own medicine – now they were being controlled.

Then there were the children whose only escape was going out every day to school.

But I was in a safe situation, living a life I used to dream about – my son safe with me, a beautiful man, a lovely new home with my boy – yet I was in a terrible place mentally. Because of the triggers.

Like many of us, I had to set up an office at home and I found it difficult to adapt, working with my family around me, worried they would judge me in my job, and I was on hyper alert at first to every word that came out of my mouth on the many calls I was now doing. But I had no choice and that's what was so difficult to deal with.

On top of this, I had a large number of staff, some who were also struggling. My role drastically changed to that of counsellor for them and it was difficult, really bloody difficult, because I didn't have a clue what was going to happen next either.

One of my most difficult challenges was when a colleague started to self-harm because she felt isolated with her controlling partner. So, I was taking on her emotions as well as my own but, in this case, I had a duty of care, it was part of my job, so there was no avoiding this scenario. Other than advising her to get help and listening to her, truly listening to her, what could I have done? It's not like I could have just bobbed round to see her. I was so frustrated as it wouldn't have happened if we weren't all locked up.

It was such a difficult time, wasn't it? The trigger had me feeling like I was climbing up a muddy hillside and my only way was back down. Well, I wasn't going to go back. I remembered the beautiful lady's funeral and how I'd felt, how it had reminded me to live.

I'd worked so hard with my Head Hooligan since then, I'd managed to tame her into being a Head Buddy. I couldn't let myself continue with debilitating anxiety taking over again. My Head Hooligan was raging. I knew I had to do something.

When I read this back to myself, I really do wonder how *I managed* to carry on. I think my mask at that time was that of platinum, it was bloody heavy but looked shiny and bright. I had to carry on for everyone else, but I had to do something to cope with the overwhelming emotions I was experiencing within.

Covid had set me right back. I had worked on myself *every day* before lockdown, but I decided I would work even harder now. I got on it day and night, through sleepless nights, so I could see, smile and enjoy my time with my family indoors. In the end, through dedication and knowing what to do, I smashed it!

I practiced mindfulness, I told myself I was safe, I looked for ways I could turn my extra energy into something positive.

I thought a lot about the news. I thought of the many women stuck in domestic violence situations whilst in lockdown. I decided I wanted to help them. So, I did my PTSD course. I thought, if I understood it, I could help them deal with the aftermath, which is sometimes the worst part of the whole deal.

Whilst doing this course, I also learnt to understand

myself and help myself. I learnt what a trigger was. I had a massive lightbulb moment realising this was why lockdown was making me feel so bad. This was why the behaviours of others could send my head into turmoil. It was all starting to make sense. I managed to claw back a sense of control.

I learnt how helpful it is to recognise your triggers; if you're not aware of them, it really is confusing, and you spend a lot of your time trying to battle the anxiety that's just drilled a hole through your belly. You waste time wondering where it came from, arguing that you felt OK a minute ago! It can also become a myriad of thoughts, thoughts that you really could do without, so understanding your triggers really can help eliminate them.

Picture this – you're having a good day; life is good and all of a sudden you get a smell of aftershave. Your stomach forms knots and you start to have a panic attack with no warning whatsoever.

If you're not aware that the aftershave you just smelt was once all you could smell whilst being attacked that is triggering your brain to recall that traumatic moment, you will panic even more, making the whole scenario much worse than it needs to be.

When you're triggered, acknowledge it. Tell yourself, 'Ah, this is a trigger. It's making me remember this scenario or that scenario and my brain is hypersensitive because of that scenario, but it's just a false alarm because all is well, I am OK, and I am safe.'

The anxiety in your belly or throat or wherever it hits you may still occur, but actually it's not real because *this is a false alarm*. You're not in that scenario, you're not in that trauma, you're OK.

Just observe your anxiety, accept it and let it settle calmly.

Acknowledge the feeling and remind yourself it's not real, telling yourself, 'It's only reacting to my brain, who thinks I'm in danger because it's looking out for me, *but I'm OK.'* Keep telling yourself that you're safe.

Look around and become aware. Take in the here and now.

Just today, when I was giving my friend some advice, she said to me, 'When your head is so deep in it, it's so hard.' I smiled and nodded. When you're resisting it and you're not addressing the real issue, then it is hard. Once you open up to change and acceptance, it's not as difficult.

She shook her head. She wasn't ready. But what she did promise was that she would try and acknowledge what I'd said; because anything is better than what goes on in our heads at times.

You *can* take yourself out of it – just for a moment –

you can.

I say this because if I can, anyone can, and it really does help to do so.

By the end of lockdown, I was the healthiest I'd been in a long time mentally.

The catastrophist in me had immediately jumped through previous triggers, and once I started to learn why they were happening and settling them down through my own new positive mindset, things started to lighten up.

I realised that my son and partner were best friends, who laughed with each other all the time.

I know that *I* could have caused a very different atmosphere if I had allowed my Head Hooligan to tell me that it was a hopeless situation. So, by me changing the way I thought and teaching my Head Hooligan that she had nothing to worry about, we came through unscathed, and she returned to being a Head Buddy.

Five Tips That Will Help You Deal with Your Triggers

1. Identify the trigger.

2. Understand what specifically triggers you. Awareness is the first step in managing triggers effectively.

3. Practise mindfulness. When triggered, focus on the

present moment, don't judge yourself. Use breathing or grounding exercises, these will help to calm your mind.

4. Create a coping plan. Develop a strategy for dealing with triggers such as distraction techniques, positive self-talk (talk with your Head Buddy, don't let her become a Head Hooligan), or reach out to a supportive friend (not the one who you only set half an hour for (wink).

5. Seek professional help. Consider therapy or counselling to go through your underlying issues contributing to the triggers. A therapist can provide personalised coping strategies and support.

6. Self-care. Prioritise self-care activities that promote emotional wellbeing – exercise, adequate sleep, healthy eating and engaging in hobbies you enjoy. Taking care of yourself can build resilience against triggers.

> "We cannot all succeed when
> half of us are held back."
>
> *Malala Yousafzai*

Chapter Six - Our Head Hooligans

By now you will have caught on to the little character who I have created to describe my overthinking. The Head Hooligan. By now you may or may not have realised that you too have your own Head Hooligan. It's sometimes a good idea to name the voice that creates your internal dialogue so you can start building a healthier relationship with it. By naming the thoughts, it makes it more personal.

My own Head Hooligan used to feel like she could just come from nowhere.

Honestly, I remember on one occasion lying in bed, having done a full body scan and then listening to some nice calming meditation, my eyes heavy and my breathing flowing beautifully, snuggling down for a lovely, relaxed sleep and BOOM – *she wasn't fucking tired.*

Then, in that moment, I heard from absolutely nowhere:

'You were shit today when you did that presentation at work.'

'Oh, go away, I am going to sleep and I'm in a really nice space here.'

I envisaged her running about in my head, dragging herself a stool to sit on, she meant business.

'You sounded a right dick.'

'Right, you are a dick, and I am going to sleep.' I wouldn't let her win.

I turned over. The beautiful comfortable space was starting to make me feel hot.

'It was shit…' I began to agree as I flopped myself onto my belly. 'I bet my new boss is regretting giving me the job.' Then I began to think about my boss's reaction to the report I had given her the other day. I could tell she wasn't happy.

I turned over again. I sighed, squeezed my eyes tight, shook my head.

I was fuming. I knew it was going to be a long night. I started to imagine how tired I was going to be at work tomorrow. I was aware that my Head Hooligan wasn't going to give me any peace.

'Please go away. I need to sleep, and you've just messed my night up and I am going to be too tired to work properly tomorrow.'

'What would you do if she asked you to leave because you're just not cutting it?'

'She's not going to do that!' I tried to convince myself. 'There are loads of times she actually praises me, and she really likes me.'

'She did *but say that presentation has put her off you and she realises you're a knob and you're not in the right*

role, you're aiming too high this time.'

I opened my eyes; she'd won, she was in and not letting go.

I was reeling in anger now. I was wide awake.

I picked up my phone and scrolled up and down a blurry Facebook, reading arguments on local sites, trying to take my mind off work, but getting emotionally embroiled in the Facebook shit I was reading.

Both conversations in my head were really unhealthy because my Head Hooligan was being a bugger in poking me into thinking I was going to lose my job. Yet I was just as bad because I was telling her to go away, but I was also listening to her and letting her take over to a point I'd stimulated my head even more by going on social media!

I have, in the past, tried to ask myself questions when my Head Hooligan starts. I have asked whether she is daydreaming. When I say daydreaming, I mean creating scenarios that are never going to happen. Is she creating scenarios to try to boost my ego by creating an unreal scene, whereby I'm having an argument that in all reality is probably never going to happen to me, but I'm smashing it, so it makes me feel boosted?

I ask if she's worried about the future – catastrophising about what isn't going to happen, imagining all sorts of scenarios that don't exist yet. How can they exist? I'm still in the time of now; the only promised time I have.

Is she ruminating about the past, changing scenarios to suit, or even making them worse than they were by adding bits in?

In the instance of my example above, she was worrying about the future. The future that didn't exist yet, because all we have is now, right now.

In reality all of them are a waste of thought. The past cannot be changed, it's gone. You can't go back and change it, no matter what your Head Hooligan says, it's really gone, nothing can take you back ever and it can't define you, but of course, experience can make you more resilient. The past has to be just that – the past.

Don't forget as well, the future doesn't exist, not only is it not promised but if you go into the future with shit thoughts, you will get a shit future, end of! If you worry about it being awful; it will be awful mainly because you feel so shit through worrying.

I realised that often I would daydream with her, my Head Hooligan. It was shocking; she wanted me to win every battle that came to me, however, the battles I had weren't real. They didn't come to fruition. They were in my head. They took a lot of energy, fucked with my head and were pointless.

What occurred to me was... I was arguing with myself.

My Head Hooligan was telling me one thing and I was arguing with her... but both of them *are me!*

Your examples might be different – you might be dropping off to sleep and that flipping gas bill pops into your head and then thoughts about how it's going to get paid and what you'll have to sacrifice in order to find the money start swimming through your mind. Then you may get in your head that the world is so unfair; everything is increasing except your wages.

Then there's the fear of the loss of connectedness, of becoming a non-person – unwanted, not respected and unvalued by anyone else, which literally threatens our wellbeing and survival; all because you're skint and going to lose the house and all its contents.

So, how do we beat our Head Hooligan?

Well, she's actually not to be beaten, she's to be loved... **she's you.**

It goes back to the same old, same old. Be aware and don't fight her. You should be kind to your Head Hooligan because, as I've just said, she is you! It's actually really awful how you shout and berate and argue with her/ yourself, and you really wouldn't talk to anyone else like that. So, be kind to her/yourself, for you both spend a lot of time in that head of yours. In addition, when she starts, ask her to be kind to you. She's a softy really, and you'll see when you ask her this, she will be.

The art is to combine you both to one level, where you both agree, and one doesn't rule the other and the only way you can do that in any relationship is through understanding each other and accepting each other.

Although we've had a volatile relationship, I've come to love my Head Hooligan. After all, she is looking out for me, she just gets carried away at times. She's just reacting to all those triggers and your bad past experiences, she's reacting to the future and tries to warn you dramatically what's coming, but she's got it totally wrong. She's a Head Hooligan not a bloody clairvoyant and, besides all that, she must be knackered. If you learn to love her and realise that subconsciously she doesn't want to hurt you, albeit she will if you let her, she will calm right down, you could even begin to love her and the things she says, she could become your Head Buddy.

If you fight with her, she will bite back. *But* she's *you*. You're fighting with yourself.

Don't allow her to self-sabotage, let you overthink negative thoughts, catastrophise, or daydream about a load of bollocks.

She doesn't need it, nor do you.

Here's an odd question – Does your Head Hooligan bring you comfort? Really think about this.

People are addicted to all sorts of things – alcohol, sex, eating, but most of all, believe it or not, the biggest addiction of all is overthinking.

For example, I talked about daydreaming (but not in the happy ethereal sense).

I have a memory of getting into bed one evening, about to listen to the Calm app, but *instead* I was happy enough to create scenarios where I came out on top.

Our neighbour has severe OCD and has a real meltdown if I park my car over a certain line that forms his driveway. He becomes abusive and rages about the car. He once knocked on the door name-calling and called the police one time too. Trigger – he sends me into a state of anxiety; therefore, I am really careful not to do this because the aftermath just isn't worth it and, the nice lady inside me, really doesn't want to send him into meltdown, imagine living in *his* head!

One night I was lying there and my Head Hooligan (are you bored of her yet?!) states:

'You've parked over his line!' (It was not over his drive!)

And even though I *knew* I hadn't, I started to worry about the consequences as though I *had.*

Say he puts my tyres down in the night, I won't be able to get to work! Remember, I wasn't even parked over the line!

What if he scratches my car? I wasn't even parked over the line!

What if he's had enough and tries to get in the house and murder me? Have I locked the door? I wasn't even parked over the line!

My Head Hooligan conjured up a scenario where I went to the front door and was greeted by the police, I was ready for them! (I must have had a good day in the office).

I had a conversation with the police lady, who I totally outsmarted with my words. I was articulate with the conversation about the neighbour.

I was so wrapped up in the story I was creating, that I felt there was no need for the Calm app.

I was actually really enjoying the thoughts; they were making me feel good. It was like my Head Hooligan was validating something for me. It's quite possible that she was letting me know that I *could* stand up for myself.

I realised, after about 10 minutes, that I was letting my Head Hooligan in, not ruminating, not catastrophising but daydreaming.

I was literally putting myself through some process by scaring myself first, then winning the battle that I was creating. It's not healthy.

I had got lost in thought and, although I was aware, I

let it continue for ages. God help those who have no self-awareness. This is how major deterioration starts. We see people who talk nonsense out loud, and we write them off as crazy. Well, we do the same, but in our heads.

This is why overthinking is addictive; it's comforting, and you do have to experience it to realise this.

I've thought about this often – how, as a little girl, I would often get in bed early just to 'think'. I would have stories in my head that I would continue every night until I created my own little soap opera. I did that for years and years, for as long as I can think back, and I guess that's where my addiction came from. It's hard to let go, but as I've become older and life has taken its dark turns, as it does occasionally, the thoughts have formed a negative pattern and affected my mental health. I am very rarely the hero in my little soap operas anymore, more a catastrophising wreck.

Anyway, I then fell asleep (after the neighbour thoughts) and woke up from a nightmare about my past and lay there in a cold sweat until my partner coughed and my world felt OK again.

This is real shit, girls, and this is where our Head Hooligans can take us, if we let them.

The fact is – overthinking actually masks the real pain that you need to deal with – such as the trauma suffered, the abuse, the attack, the chaotic household as a child, the bully at school. In overthinking you're masking all of these things, and they all need dealing with somehow. Your Head Hooligan, therefore, is actually trying to protect you from facing that, and all the time you're trying to fix a made-up problem that's not even there whilst avoiding the ones that really are there.

Take a moment to think about what has *really* happened to you to get you to this place, this place of chaos.

Think back to your life as a little girl – was it easy or was it chaos?

Go back to your teenage years – did you fit in; did you experience bullying?

Were you treated differently from your siblings?

Did you feel neglect from a parent or carer?

Have you experienced rape?

Did you experience sexual abuse?

Because whatever has traumatised you in the past, if it wasn't dealt with effectively at the time or later on, then that's one of the causes, if not all of the causes, of your Head Hooligan – she is a symptom of your inner fear. When we've experienced trauma, our mind can't let go until it's all straightened out, until we've worked on the feelings, accepted them and moved forward.

My Head Hooligan still goes on the occasional rampage, and I suppose she always will but, almost immediately, I'm aware, I catch her, I accept her, love her and she calms much quicker now than she ever did. I often roll my eyes and say, 'Be a darling!' and she is.

And there are times I literally laugh out loud at her, and she realises she's being a dick and pipes right down.

Sometimes, when I hear her voice, she isn't even talking like a Head Hooligan anymore, she is a Head Buddy. Her voice is a positive, supportive one. It is a much more peaceful place inside my head now.

How to Tame Your Head Hooligan

Be aware of your feelings and what triggers them.

When you're hearing the negative chatter, do not react to her.

Stay calm no matter what she's telling you (remember it's you and you're probably panicking, catastrophising or ruminating).

Ask her to be kind to you.

Change the thoughts around to positive thoughts.

For example, if your Head Hooligan is saying, '*You're not good enough*', then you pause before asking her to be kind, you have time to reframe it into something like

'You are capable and worthy of success and will continue to improve'.

It's about shifting your perspective to focus on solutions and opportunities rather than letting your Head Hooligan dwell on setbacks or limitations. It's a scientific fact that the more you repeat the positive self-talk, the more your subconscious will record it as facts.

Another example, this time for you ladies who smoke and want to give up.

Your Head Hooligan will beat you up massively for this one, because it is a habit that makes the smoker feel constantly torn between hate and addiction.

Can you hear her now?

'You're killing yourself!

It's so uneducated to smoke nowadays!

Lung cancer is on the up.'

You already know this, but addiction takes over. If you pause, even as you're smoking, giving her no reaction, and then say this aloud: 'I don't smoke!' Say it daily. It can help reinforce positive behaviour and beliefs and influence your subconscious over time. It's better than her telling you you're going to bloody die when you feel guilty enough. And one day hopefully you'll have a lit cigarette in your hand and wonder what the hell you're doing... because you *don't smoke*.

If you ask your Head Hooligan to be kind, she'll remind you that you don't smoke. She loves you really, because she is *you*.

The quote below made me smile.

"Trust the overthinker who tells you they love you. They have, most assuredly, thought of every reason not to."

LK Pilgrim

Chapter Seven - The Power of Here and Now

It's taken me years to actually grasp this context. I said in my introduction about the number of self-help books I've read, but until I actually got the message and felt the message, none of them clicked. Don't get me wrong, they were very comforting at the time, and I did take a few bits from each. It was only when I realised, they were all saying the same thing in different ways that they clicked. So, I would love *you* to grasp it through my book. The messages I heard were:

Be aware.

Feel here and now.

Stay mindful.

Be present.

Be non-judgemental to your thoughts.

Accept all that is happening to you.

Be an observer.

Easy to say, but not easy to practice unless you absolutely grasp it, realise it and feel it. Not one of the books said to carry on as it is and you'll feel better, or ignore it and it will go away, because it certainly won't.

The practice of absolutely being here, in the present

moment, means no thoughts of the past and no catastrophising about the future. The realisation that whilst you concentrate hard on the here and now, your Head Hooligan either goes to sleep or goes with you on the present journey, gives you headspace, allowing actual real solutions to appear because your Head Hooligan has previously been blocking them.

Whilst being in the present moment you have to be non-judgemental or that will be the bait for your Head Hooligan. It's about letting go of the judgements that arise in your head with every experience you have. It's about accepting ourselves, and if she does bob in, it's about being kind to her and not telling her to fuck off. Ask her to be kind instead. She will and can turn it round into positivity.

It's about truly immersing ourselves in the present moment without evaluating it, arguing with it or denying it. Embracing 'what is' and giving yourself that headspace to breathe. She *will* bob in occasionally and she will cause you anxiety, see if you can just observe the thought and feeling, once observed, let it go and bring yourself back into the here and now, always remembering the thoughts are not real, nor is the anxiety that follows them (although they feel very bloody real). If you can, listen to your own breath.

The power of *now* shows you that every minute you spend overthinking about the future or ruminating about the past, is a minute wasted, and the way our Head Hooligans work, those minutes soon add up to hours, days, and weeks. Sadly, in some cases, years and years have been lost by overthinking.

I've already pointed out it is addictive, and you know the consequences of addiction. But you can't go cold turkey with thinking – it's impossible because we're required to think to live. Can you imagine, as good as it sounds, going through a whole day without thinking negative thoughts? Negative thoughts can be needed, they are helpful at times in making decisions. But too many are just exhausting.

It takes time, of course, to break the habit, you have to really want to. You have to commit time and effort, because overthinking is not just going to go away one day, but you can turn your thoughts into more positive ones, not ruminate on the negative ones.

I can't be in the here and now yet, all day long. I can't even do it for hours at a time (until yesterday), but for me it has to be baby steps because my Head Hooligan is a bugger as we know. For short periods throughout the day:

I allow myself to *listen* and to *hear*.

I teach myself to feel what *now* feels like.

I allow myself to become *still*.

I really smell and taste the moment.

Now that I have done all of the above, I am totally aware when I get a 'thought', and almost instantaneously now I tell myself, 'I'm having a thought, it's OK.'

Sometimes, though, even now, it's like giving in to that cigarette you keep promising to give up and sometimes, I'll say, 'Ah it's OK, come in, my little Head Hooligan, I've missed you. I don't actually feel that bad today, so I will be able to cope with anything you have to offer!' That's when the deterioration sets in. I start to go downhill, regressing into that negative spiral that I so don't want. Or do I?

Let's talk about the ego for a minute, whose job it is to make you feel important, *her* survival depends on it, and *she* needs a negative stimulus so that she has something to do.

The ego from a spiritual perspective is not much different and is said to be the part of the mind that controls its thinking and your behaviour, so as an overthinker the ego forms allies with your Head Hooligan (best friends for life) and will cause all the arguments in your head. If you really think about it (I'm trying to get you to *not* overthink), nearly every single thought you have has the ego in the background.

The thoughts of 'I'm not good enough' even come from

the ego, as you push yourself to be better than everyone else, even if it's going against your beautiful grain.

Whichever way you look at it – whether you're the victim who constantly wants sympathy about how bad your life has been so far, or the complainer of just about everything that happens in your life – it's your ego wanting some sort of attention as it tries to validate you and make you the most important person in the world.

The victim with their 'I'm worse off than anybody' scenario comes from the ego, because it makes them feel better when others validate them. So, her ego is saying, 'I'm the best victim in the world.'

Then there is the complainer who complains just about everything. Well, she is actually trying to compete with the people she is complaining to, with an 'I'll show them' mentally. Show them what? Show them how much better than them she is.

It makes them feel like a better person if they come out on top, boosting that ego considerably. It's another addictive pattern of wanting validation. It's so sad when you think that actually all we need to do is really love ourselves.

A lot of your overthinking comes from your very own ego. When you tell yourself that and drop her for a minute, your outlook becomes very different, and you start to feel peace. At my stage of life now I just want to feel peace, so feeling peace versus feeling the need to be the best or be right, is a winner every day for me.

My friend said to me when I told her this, 'Aren't you just being submissive?'

I'm absolutely *not* being submissive. *This is powerful*. Powerful to not overthink and feed the ego. I'm taking control and seeing my life as it is, in the here and now. But my friend wasn't ready at that time.

Call it what you will; but dropping your ego is the best way to enrich your personal wellbeing and, in doing so, promoting your self-esteem and productivity whilst you will enjoy a fuller life.

After all, isn't this what we all want, ladies?

Ask yourself, when you're next wanting retaliation or revenge for that argument that's been brewing, do I want to be right or happy? Your Head Hooligan will tell you, *'Put the bastards straight!'* Well, that feels a lot of energy to me.

If you're wanting revenge, tune into your Head Buddy (the more you do this the easier it will become).

'The best way to have any kind of revenge is to love yourself. Be kind to yourself here, you deserve to be a happier, calmer person. What someone else thinks about you, is their business, not yours,' your Head Buddy will

Lynette Heywood

say.

Forget the scenario, that's happened, it's in the past.

Your ego will make you want to prove that you know better and want to come out feeling on top, making you the best. Whether you're right or wrong is irrelevant. You want to prove that you're better than the other person involved and even deeper than that, you need to prove that your existence here on earth is valid. It's your ego goading you all the time as she needs you to be important and better than anyone else in the world. She is, therefore, causing you no end of stress. She thrives off your Head hooligan; so, it's time to let her go.

The ego has a huge contribution to your future thoughts.

What if I fail? What if I lose my job? What if he dumps me?

If I fail, I won't be the best.

If I lose my job, everyone will doubt me, and I won't be the best.

I'm not the best if he dumps me.

When you come into the present moment, your ego doesn't play any part, you don't need her because once you connect with who you really are, you will feel your own self-worth.

Yesterday was probably my greatest achievement in staying still. I did it for a full morning and had a lovely peaceful day with my Head Buddy.

I'm always good at staying in the moment first thing, because it is my favourite time of the day. I'm up early, 5.30am sometimes, and I have a couple of hours before the world wakes up. I always feel totally safe and almost untouchable because everyone else is asleep. It's usually once the day kicks in and people awake that I become out of sorts.

I always do my self-care in the morning as I know it sets me up for the day ahead; it's so important for me because I don't cope very well internally if I don't.

I always have my coffee in the garden or, if it's raining, I will sit in the garage with the back door open. I love watching the garden getting drenched, I love the way the rain touches everything.

We have the most beautiful garden with a big silver birch tree whose branches fill the whole garden. It looks magical as you have to lower your head to look underneath the branches. It's a beautiful marquee of pale green leaves at the moment.

I really, really am so grateful for those small moments. Feelings of gratitude can boost serotonin and activate part of our brain to produce the pleasure chemical dopamine.

So, it's not just a spiritual belief that gratitude is good for you, it's a hard fact that it is.

On a very good day, I wake up *in* self-care, feeling that feeling in my belly of being so grateful to have even woken up. I will grab my Air Pods and before I'm out of bed, I am listening to either Gabby Bernstein, Wayne Dyer, Ekhart Tolle or Louise Hay; depending on what my needs are.

If I want to feel inspired and reminded, I listen to Gabby.

If I want soothing and wisdom, I listen to Wayne.

If I want to feel present, I will listen to Ekhart.

If I want to enhance the positivity, I listen to Louise.

I will meditate for at least ten minutes a day. I try to be consistent too because if I only do this when I'm feeling shit, it all starts to remind me of feeling shit. It's important to do it all the time or as often as you can. It's like going to the gym; you feel amazing once you've been, but once you start to trail off your old sluggish ways and negative feelings return.

Every evening, I do a meditation from the Calm app and when my Head Hooligan tries to rear her head, I will always do a body scan so I can become aware and notice any tension in any area of my body.

Below is a body scan for you to follow or you can go on YouTube and find one from there. Try it and see if you can do your full body. If I do one of these in bed, I'm usually fast asleep before I get to my toes. Remember, if your Head Hooligan pops into your head, acknowledge the thought, don't judge it or her, accept it, then just observe the thought and let her go and direct your thoughts back to wherever you're up to in your body scan.

First of all, actually give yourself permission to take a few minutes out of your busy head.

It's really OK to have time to do this.

This is a very quick body scan, just so you have an idea about what to do, but you can focus on one area for as long as you want to.

If you can, read it a couple of times and practice it before you give it a go.

Ready?

Find a comfortable position and lay your hands by your side (pause).

Close your eyes gently and allow yourself to relax.

Soften your shoulders.

Take five deep breaths.

Feel your breath as it enters your body.

Feel it as it leaves your body.

Now bring your attention to your head.

Feeling your scalp, breathe into your scalp, imagine it softening.

Breathe in and breathe out.

Now feel your forehead and your face.

Allow all the muscles in your forehead and face to soften.

Breathe in and breathe out.

Focus now on your neck and your shoulders, notice the feelings here.

Soften your shoulders as you breathe out.

Breathe in and breathe out.

Move that awareness to your arms.

Move it all the way down to your wrists.

Now truly feel your palms.

You might feel a tingling sensation, let it be.

Breathe in and breathe out.

Now move your awareness to your fingers.

Gently move your focus to your back. If you notice any tension here, direct the breath into that area.

Let your back soften and breathe into it.

Breathe in and breathe out.

Now into your belly, be aware of it rising and falling as you breathe in and out.

In and out.

In and out.

Scan your pelvis and hips.

Move your attention all the way down your legs to your feet, letting them relax and become soft.

Breathe in and breathe out.

Settle into the stillness that comes about by paying attention to your body, bit by bit.

When you're ready, wriggle your fingers and toes and come back to the room, gently opening your eyes.

*"The true definition of mental illness is
when the majority of your time is spent in
the past or future, but rarely living
in the realism of NOW."*

Shannon L. Alder

Chapter Eight - Treatments for Trauma

We've looked at being in the present moment, which is the best way to ensure you're living in the now and experiencing your life instead of spending your time constantly worrying.

This will help your overthinking and your anxiety and bring you away from those fear-based, negative thoughts.

But if you *have* suffered from trauma, no matter how big the trauma, because it's your perception, then there are other avenues for you to pursue. I said earlier – please talk with your GP and tell him/her what you're going through.

You could also try any of the following:

Hypnosis

The use of hypnosis in trauma can be beneficial, there has been much research into the use of hypnosis with remarkable results. You must be aware, though, that the thought of losing control i.e., revisiting the traumatic event, could make you extremely anxious at the very idea of it, so just make sure you and your Head Hooligan have the confidence or ability to deal with the re-presented trauma.

Cognitive Behaviour Therapy

This is used a lot for treating trauma. It gives you the opportunity to understand what you are suffering from and to talk it through with someone who understands.

A good therapist will help you to identify your thoughts and the behaviours associated with your trauma. They will help you to reframe and alter your behaviour in steps so that you can influence your thoughts and behaviour for the better.

Unlocking Positive Memories

Depending on the severity of the trauma, positive memories are locked away in your mind. They are there but you're unable to get at them. To bring those positives alive, write about them for a couple of minutes a day. As you start to write, your positive memories will flow. If you can't be bothered writing about them, start to talk about them.

Managing Irritability

So many times, we get pissed off as women and it can depend on the time of the month. Our hormones are fricking raging out of control, but sometimes it's not hormone-related, it's the fact that we're women and we're supposed to 'do it all' and with so many demands on our time, it's no wonder that sometimes we get irritable.

I don't express anger very often, well not in the conventional way, but I sulk or deal with it internally. Many people when they're angry due to trauma act it out by screaming at the kids or a partner, leaving them feeling even worse later on.

When you notice your first signs of anger (if you're aware, you will), you can either come back to the here and now or imagine a set of traffic lights in front of you.

The light is red, shout 'Stop!' to yourself.

The light turns to amber – ask yourself if you're really justified in your anger, whether it's really the end of the world.

The light goes to green – grab your Calm app and meditate instead of reacting outwardly.

If you don't have access to any apps, a simple technique for grounding yourself, which works just as well is, the **Hear, See, Feel** technique.

Hear: Listen to the sounds around you, such as the birds singing or the hum of The Washing. (Let's face it, it's always on) Focusing on these sounds will anchor you in the present moment.

See: Look around and notice five things you can see.

Pay attention to details like colours, shapes and textures to bring your focus on what's going on outside you, instead of in that head of yours.

Feel: Tune into your body and identify four things you can physically feel, such as the sensation of your feet on the ground or the texture of your clothing. Again, this helps to ground you in your physical experience.

By engaging your senses, you can bring yourself back to the present moment and alleviate feelings of anxiety. This will also keep your Head Hooligan at bay.

Positive Affirmations

It's so important and possible to retrain your brain from thinking negative thoughts. Positive affirmations help us to do this. I can honestly say that when I stick with my positive affirmations, I do feel a difference, and if I do them daily, my good days turn into good weeks and so on.

For the next seven days, try the following affirmations, saying them out loud, looking in the mirror if you can (this can be uncomfortable at first), if not, say them and mean them.

I am enough.

I believe in my dreams, myself and all that I am.

I love myself for who I am.

I create my own happiness.

My life is filled with an abundance of goodness.

My challenges are actually opportunities.

I am beautiful just the way I am.

Gratitude

Being grateful for what you have is a sure way to help with your feelings of anxiety. Even if you have PTSD, there is always something to be grateful for.

However, there are many times you may feel so badly done to that you can't see the wood for the trees. It can be so difficult to keep your head above the paraphyte that it can feel impossible to find the things that you *do* have, and you *are* grateful for, *but* that's what you should try and do even when you're feeling the shittiest.

As I said before, being grateful and having that strong feeling of gratitude actually rewires the brain, making your life so much easier to cope with, because it is possible to change your whole attitude.

Being grateful can give you those positive feelings of pleasure, happiness and wellbeing. You *can* mend that head of yours.

Think about it, even if you're in a bad place now or you've just had a trigger, just stop and think for a moment.

Right now, as you read this book, at the very minimal *you're breathing* (I hope), and I say minimal because if that's all you think you've got then *wow,* you're here and you have the honour of being alive. I can never get over the fact our bodies are working hard in the background to keep us going day in, day out.

How often do you acknowledge that and actually feel truly grateful for it?

It's important that you remember (no matter how bad you're feeling), what is going good for you at the moment. If it's absolutely shit at the moment for you, remember – you can breathe and you wake up in the morning.

Can you see? Are you lucky enough to see the oranges in the autumn, the white in the winter and are able to stare at the blue skies in the summer?

I am so grateful for my sight, or I wouldn't be able to write my books and see the colours changing in nature.

Can you hear? Can you hear children laughing in the distance as they enjoy their playtime? Can you listen to your favourite music when you're feeling down? Can you hear the much-needed silence? As I write, the rain is banging away on the corrugated roof of the conservatory and I am warm and cosy, sitting here tapping away.

Can you feel? Does stroking a dog, a cat or horse boost your mood and ease depression?

I love the feel of material on my palms, it's a comfort thing from childhood, I still love the feeling it gives me.

Go and grab a pen and a bit of paper.

Write down ten things you are truly grateful for. Smile and appreciate what you do have. I bet you will feel a tiny bit better – go on, I dare you!

I'll write mine down as they appear in my head right now.

I woke up this morning in my beautiful bed, all cosy and warm.

I had a shower with hot water and soap.

My partner makes me laugh every day.

My children are all healthy.

My mum is safe and well.

I have really lovely genuine friends.

I have the tools to help me feel better and can use them every day.

I am safe.

I have the most beautiful garden.

My breath never lets me down.

Reiki

Beneficial in so many ways, Reiki is a natural way

to reduce stress, pain relief, emotional healing and enhanced wellbeing. It involves the trained individual placing their hands on the client's body and encouraging healthy energy flow.

My friend has set up her own business to help people who want to approach improving their mental health the natural way. Her reviews and feedback are amazing. I have had a few sessions with her and can honestly say it's one of the few occasions my mind actually stops thinking yet sees the most beautiful colours. The feeling of calm around me is just beautiful and I carry it for days.

Remember, we can choose how we want to feel, if we really put our minds to it. Negative thoughts are bad for you. Good thoughts are good for you. If you kept eating food that made you feel ill, you'd stop eating it. So, stop those negative thoughts by working hard and make a commitment to help yourself feel better.

You can either stay stuck where it's easier in some respects but with long term damage. Without working on you and your Head Hooligan, your trauma, your anxiety, you are never ever going to wake up one day and say, 'What was all that about? Because I feel better, and everything has gone away.'

All it is, is a change of habit. We diet often enough (well, some of us do), but this time it's a diet for the soul.

You can't be on a diet forever, but you can adjust your lifestyle so you don't have to diet but can still be healthy.

The same should be said for the way we talk to ourselves. Why are there so many programmes about lifestyles and diets, but it's pretty much taboo to talk about our innermost thoughts and how miserable they can make us? Tackling overthinking is the same as tackling overeating – we make adjustments, we set boundaries, we recognise we may have a bad day, but then we can get ourselves back on track.

Start by putting some little steps in day by day and you'll soon see a difference.

I love this quote:

> *"When all you know is fight or flight, red flags and butterflies all feel the same."*
>
> *Cindy Cherie*

Chapter Nine – Woman Up

So, ladies, we are strong. Men wouldn't get out of bed if they had to go through what we go through daily. You've seen them when they've got a cold – never mind stomach cramps, backache, woozy head, can't concentrate, cry one minute, scream the next.

There are so many times I've had to go home from work to get changed because my period has been so heavy. The physical pain for us can also be horrendous. Some say, 'You're not ill, it's just a period!' But if you look up illness, it states: 'A disease or period of sickness affecting the body and or mind.'

For one week of the month, we *are ill,* yet we didn't stay off school and we don't stay off work. Jesus, boys, you wouldn't believe what we see down that toilet at times. Still to this day (because I don't even know where I'm at in the stage of perimenopause, I'm still as regular as I have been since I was eleven years old) I do Taggart's Scottish accent and say, 'There's been a murder!'

We go to school and try our utmost to fit in with our peers and be popular, all the while feeling lost and left out if we don't get invited to this or that, or the other girls don't want us in their clique. That's when the questioning starts in your head. *Why me? What don't they like?* You know what's sad, really sad? You're still only a baby!

Then there's the boys in school who give you a harder time than the girls if they're not attracted to you. It's a shame because early on they're taught from ingrained and old beliefs, that girls are the weaker sex, and they treat them secondary, even from this early age.

I do hope it's changed somewhat in *today's* school because we are seeing more females doing what was once a 'male activity'. Just look at our England Women's Football Team; go, lionesses, you show them!

We go through childbirth – that's after carrying our little bundle of joy for nine months – another huge hormone blow to our bodies and minds. The fear and worry, as well as the excitement for women, is second-to-none, as soon as we get that 'positive', so begins the Mummy Nightmare – the worry about losing this bundle. It's absolutely terrifying for every pregnant lady as it's always at the back of her mind that she may have a miscarriage or a stillbirth or a poorly baby. It never goes away, as you'll all know if you chose to have children.

Once we have a little bundle of joy, with only half of our bodies intact, on we go, deprived of sleep, with a cloud for a brain whilst this baby depends on us for its every breath.

Some of us then get postpartum depression (PPD), which is a recognised illness, but unlike any other illness you can't take to your bed with this one, because there is a new-born depending on you for its every breath. We are instilled with 'just get on with it' passed down from our grandmas and their grandmas. My mum said the other day, 'That bloody menopause is all over social media, it's in your face!' I replied with, 'Yes, it needs to be. So many women suffer and have different responses so sharing our experiences can make it easier.'

When I explained that women are able to cut down their hours at work because of the debilitation it can cause, she said, 'God! Your grandma would go mad; it was never ever spoken about in our day – they just got on with it.'

God bless them for having to suffer alone and in silence. Imagine being an anxious, empathic overthinker in those days, or suffering with PPD and having no outlet, no medication, no tools to feel better.

It must have been horrendous, but of course 'they just got on with it'.

Imagine in the 'old days' when they just 'got on with it' – having surgery without anaesthetic. Just because they *did* in those days, doesn't mean we have to *now*! New medications, awareness and being able to talk about things which cause us suffering are *good* things. I dislike hearing things like: 'Well, when I was growing up, we had *ice* inside our windows, and we didn't moan about gas prices like you are today!' OMG should we all suffer, despite working harder than ever, with the massive cost of living, and just accept that it is OK in 2024 to be freezing in our own homes?!

So, the baby is here, now what? Depending on how we feel, some of us want to go back to work, some of us don't. Some of us don't have a choice, some do. Then the judging starts. 'You can't leave your baby', 'What did you have her for if you just want to work?',' She's too young to leave at nursery' – as if we don't feel bad enough!

The decision is usually always on the mother to sort out the childcare, set up a nursery, visit the ones we like the look of and reject the ones we don't. More often than not, it is the mother who has to take the days off work when Baby is poorly. Most workplaces offer split parental leave now, which is amazing and really works for some couples who share everything.

Then there is the guilt of going to work and leaving your baby. Whilst we have every right to be as successful as our male peers, it's still a drain on our feelings and emotions.

There are many reasons why a woman decides to return to work after having a baby. It could be money, but it could also be about her own career, her mental health, what she enjoys, how she wants to bring up her child. Whatever the reason, the mother is often torn and questions whether they're a good mum or a good worker or are they failing at both. Returning to work takes balance and lots of guts and it feels impossible most of the time to get that balance right.

Girls, please just stop for a moment and recognise yourself for all you go through. My goodness, what an achievement. We never get congratulated or acknowledged because we're females, it's just what we do – but it's bloody amazing, all of it.

A photograph that always gets to me, is that of 'The Migrant Mother'. This photograph symbolises the hunger and poverty endured by many Americans during the Great Depression.

The migrant mother sits there in poverty whilst her children still depend on her. It tells you a hundred stories just by looking at it.

'The migrant mother's furrowed brow and hand placement suggests anxiety and worry about her duties as a mother to nurture and protect her children. Her expression and juxtaposition with her children and clothing indicates that the family is overcome by circumstances they cannot control, thus removing any blame from the mother. The children leaning on their mother depicts the

*mother as the children's pillar of strength.' *Wikipedia*

Did she give up? *Never!* The photographer who took the photograph (Dorothea Lange) wrote this about Florence Owen Thompson (the migrant mother):

I was following instinct, not reason; I drove into that wet and soggy camp and parked my car like a homing pigeon. I saw and approached the hungry and desperate mother, as if drawn by a magnet. I do not remember how I explained my presence or my camera to her, but I do remember she asked me no questions. I made five exposures, working closer and closer from the same direction.

I did not ask her name or her history. She told me her age, that she was 32. She said that they had been living on frozen vegetables from the surrounding fields, and birds that the children killed. She had just sold the tyres from her car to buy food. There she sat in that lean-to tent [shed] with her children huddled around her and seemed to know that my pictures might help her, and so she helped me. There was a sort of equality about it. The pea crop at Nipomo had frozen and there was no work for anybody. But I did not approach the tents and shelters of other stranded pea-pickers. It was not necessary; I knew I had recorded the essence of my assignment.

There was a sort of equality about it that got me. Two

women from vastly different worlds, knowing that the other woman could help, sums it up for me.

Back to my point.

When we are back at work, worn out, knackered and guilt-riddled, we find that we are still treated less of a being by certain men at work who are misogynistic and insistent on objectifying women... because, of course, we're one big ball of pussy with no brains in our heads. Again, this is not all men but believe me it still happens.

And if that's not enough, the kids grow up and you start worrying about different things – where they are, if they're safe. Then along come the grandkids – grandkids come with something different... the fucking menopause.

I am worn out being a woman.

But we have perimenopause, heavy periods, no periods, light periods, don't-know-if-you're-coming-or-going periods. We want sex but it's not going so well down there, so we need cream to make it doable. If we don't want sex that's OK, but that doesn't go without the guilt you feel for your other half and the fear of him leaving you for the supermodel that lives next door-but-one. 'Thanks, Grandma!' your generation and that before has ingrained in us that 'we have to please our man when he wants pleasing'! You have to do no such thing, and a good man will stand by you for who you are, not how often you're lifting up your nightie.

During menopause your head is like a sieve, not remembering anything, but we still go to work, and we still try and hold our families together. It never ends.

I've spoken about mothers a lot and our children, but there are those beautiful souls who are not blessed with children and the other gorgeous ladies who choose not to be. Why other people feel the need to ask why you haven't got children is beyond me. 'Was it a choice or…?' Like is it their business? And to have to keep having periods which remind you that you can't have children or that you aren't sure yet and there's pressure or that you've chosen not to, and you *still* have to go through this mess every month.

Being the woman at work without children and everyone is talking about their family-busy weekends or they expect you to be able to always work the Christmas shifts because you don't have children, which is true, but you have a right to time off too, you may have other loved ones you want to spend Christmas with, other commitments or just want to spend the day on your own, not at work!

And I've not thrown in any problems here, this is all just the norm.

Think about what you have gone through and how you got here today, I bet some of your stories make mine look an Enid Blyton book (she wrote some amazing fairy tales).

Think about how you have managed. Think about what your coping strategies were, because they've obviously worked. But now you're left feeling weary. When in actual fact you should be celebrating – all the time without realising it, you were 'womaning up'. The statement 'man up', according to the Oxford dictionary, means 'to demonstrate toughness or courage when faced with a difficult situation.'

The term actually comes from the sub-language of American football where it originally referred to man to man defence; later taking a more general idea of resilience in the face of adversity.

Ladies, it's a known fact that women have reported a more complex history of childhood adversities than males. Exposure to adversities in childhood is strongly associated with poorer mental health and poorer social and emotional outcomes in adulthood.

Yet, we are more resilient, which is a fact that has been scientifically proven. As I have just made the point, we have so much more to cope with than men. So please don't tell us to 'man up'. We were born to be the stronger, more resilient, of the sexes... So, bring it on!

Thank you for reading.

Hopefully you've read, you've recognised, you've

related to, my words. Hopefully you will know that you're not alone.

I hope you've taken something from this book, but if you haven't – I hope I've given you something to smile about as well as contemplate your own worth and how bloody wonderful you are.

Or... you think I am totally bloody bonkers and have thrown the book in the black bag for the charity shop.

My message to you is: Whatever your story, however loudly your Head Hooligan shouts at you, whether you have PTSD or not, you can make a difference to how you live your life and you can start today.

Only you *create your own nightmares, and only* you *can stop them by making friends with your Head Hooligan and, in doing so, making friends with yourself.*

For she is you, beautiful you.

Resources

I have listed some resources for you to google, they might help with some of the topics you've read:

Women's Aid UK – Help for women and children

Mind UK – Mental health resource

NHS – Post Traumatic Stress Disorder

Refuge.org – Help for women and children

Violet Moon Facebook – Reiki Practitioner

Books:

The Myth of Normal by Gabor Mate

Become an Empowered Empath by Wendy D' Rosa

You can Heal your Life by Louise Hay

The Power of Now by Eckhart Tolle

Anything by Wayne Dyer

I could go on forever …